AAT

Qualifications and Credit Framework (QCF)

LEVEL 3 DIPLOMA IN ACCOUNTING

(QCF)

QUESTION BANK

Cash Management

2011 Edition

First edition 2010

Second edition July 2011

ISBN 9780 7517 9761 9

(Previous ISBN 9780 7517 8599 9)

British Library Cataloguing-in-Publication Data
A catalogue record for this book is available from the British
Library

Published by

BPP Learning Media Ltd
BPP House
Aldine Place
London W12 8AA

www.bpp.com/learningmedia

Printed in the United Kingdom

CONTENTS

INTRODUCTION

This is BPP Learning Media's AAT Question Bank for Cash Management. It is part of a suite of new ground-breaking resources produced by BPP Learning Media for the AAT's assessments under the qualification and credit framework.

The Cash Management assessment will be **computer assessed**. As well as being available in the traditional paper format, this **Question Bank is available in an online format** where all questions and assessments are presented in a **style which mimics the style of the AAT's assessments**. BPP Learning Media believe that the best way to practise for an online assessment is in an online environment. However, if you are unable to practise in the online environment you will find that all tasks in the paper Question Bank have been written in a style that is as close as possible to the style that you will be presented with in your online assessment.

This Question Bank has been written in conjunction with the BPP Text, and has been carefully designed to enable students to practise all of the learning outcomes and assessment criteria for the units that make up Cash Management. It is fully up-to-date as at July 2011 and reflects both the AAT's unit guide and the specimen assessment provided by the AAT.

This Question Bank contains these key features:

- Tasks corresponding to each chapter of the Text. Some tasks are designed for learning purposes, others are of assessment standard

- The AAT's specimen assessment and answers for Cash Management and further practice assessments

The emphasis in all tasks and assessments is on the practical application of the skills acquired.

If you have any comments about this book, please e-mail suedexter@bpp.com or write to Sue Dexter, Publishing Director, BPP Learning Media Ltd, BPP House, Aldine Place, London W12 8AA.

Question bank

Cash Management Question Bank

Chapter 1

Task 1.1

You work in a small business which installs fire alarms. As the only member of the accounts department, you report directly to the proprietor, Mr Blaze. One day, you find the following long note from Mr Blaze on your table.

'I've been to the bank and asked them to lend me some money. I've always had money in the bank, but because the loan is to acquire some new equipment, the bank wants a full set of accounts. The manager asked for Income Statements (profit and loss accounts) and a Cash Flow statement. He then started jabbering on in jargon I didn't understand: something about *cash operating cycle times*, as he said they were relevant. I also said we were a profitable business. Then he said he needed some ideas as to how *liquid* we are. I said we were a solid company, we've been trading for many years. He said I'd better chat to an accountant. Please help!'

Choose from the picklist to complete the following sentences.

The cash operating cycle time is the	period between cash being paid for purchases and cash received for sales
	inventory (stock) turnover period plus receivables' (debtors') payment period less payables' (creditors') payment period

Liquid assets include	cash and short-term investments
	cash and receivables (debtors)
	cash, receivables (debtors) and inventory (stock)

Task 1.2

During the year ending 30 June a business made sales of £2,600,000 and its cost of sales totalled £1,800,000. At 30 June there was inventory (stock) of £250,000, receivables (debtors) of £550,000 and payables (creditors) of £200,000.

What is the cash operating cycle of the business, in days?

A   128 days
B   169 days
C   87 days
D   15 days

Task 1.3

Kitten Ltd buys raw materials on three months' credit, holds them in store for four months and then issues them to production. The production cycle is a couple of days, and then finished goods are held for one month before they are sold. Receivables (debtors) are normally allowed two months' credit.

What is Kitten Ltd's cash operating cycle in months?

A   1 month
B   2 months
C   3 months
D   4 months

Task 1.4

A business has a cash operating cycle of 76 days. This is based on inventory (stock) turnover period of 65 days, receivables' (debtors') collection period of 55 days and payables' (creditors') payment period of 44 days. The Finance Director of the business wants to improve this.

Which of the following will have the effect of shortening the cash operating cycle of the business?

A   Taking advantage of early settlement discounts offered by suppliers

B   Offering an early settlement discount to customers

C   Increasing the cash balance held in the business's current account

D   Increasing the credit terms offered to customers from 30 days to 60 days

Task 1.5

A business has an inventory (stock) turnover period of 45 days, receivables' (debtors') collection period of 40 days and payables' (creditors') payment period of 60 days. The business has launched several new product ranges which will increase the inventory turnover period by 9 days and because of the new mix of customers the average receivables' collection period will be 46 days. Supplier payments will be unaffected.

What is the cash operating cycle of the business before and after the planned changes?

	Before	After
A	145 days	40 days
B	25 days	40 days
C	145 days	160 days
D	25 days	160 days

Task 1.6

Select from the picklists to complete the following sentences.

Over-trading occurs when a business has [too much/too little] working capital.

Over-capitalisation occurs when a business has [too much/too little] working capital.

Chapter 2

Task 2.1

Selecting from the picklists complete the following sentences:

If a business makes a profit this means that [its cash inflows are greater than its cash outflow/its revenue is greater than its expenses].

Cash flow and profit will [normally/not normally] be the same figure for a period.

•••

Task 2.2

Give FIVE examples of types of reasons why there might be a difference between the profit that a business makes and its cash balance.

1

2

3

4

5

•••

Task 2.3

Given below is the forecast Income Statement (profit and loss account) for a business for the three months ending 31 December together with forecast Statements of Financial Position (balance sheets) at that date and also at the previous 30 September.

Forecast Income Statement for the three months ending 31 December

	£'000
Revenue (Turnover)	860
Cost of sales	(600)
Gross profit	260
Depreciation	(20)
Overheads	(100)
Operating profit	140

Forecast Statements of Financial Position

	31 December		30 September	
	£'000	£'000	£'000	£'000
Non-current (fixed) assets		1,050		760
Current assets:				
Inventory (stock)	100		100	
Receivables (debtors)	85		45	
Cash	10		10	
	195		155	
Payables (creditors)	100		75	
Accruals of overheads	45		40	
	145		115	
Net current assets		50		40
		1,100		800
Share capital		600		600
Retained earnings		500		200
		1,100		800

Calculate the actual cash receipts and cash payments for the quarter to 31 December.

	£'000
Sales receipts	
Purchase payments	
Overhead payments	

Task 2.4

The net book value of non-current (fixed) assets on 1 January was £125,000 and the statement of financial position (balance sheet) at 31 December shows non-current assets of £152,000. During the year £12,500 depreciation was charged. There were no non-current asset disposals.

What was the cash paid to acquire non-current assets in the year ended 31 December?

A   £12,500
B   £14,500
C   £27,000
D   £39,500

....

Task 2.5

A business decides to sell one of its machines. The machine being sold originally cost £64,400. At the date of disposal, accumulated depreciation on the machine amounts to £38,640. The machine is sold for £23,800.

What was the profit or loss on disposal of the machine?

A   £1,960 profit

B   £1,960 loss

C   £14,840 profit

D   £14,840 loss

....

Task 2.6

A business decides to sell one of its buildings which originally cost £105,000 and on which, at the date of disposal, accumulated depreciation amounted to £48,500. The sale generated a profit on disposal of £35,000.

What were the cash proceeds on disposal of the building?

A   £21,500

B   £56,500

C   £70,000

D   £91,500

....

Chapter 3

Task 3.1

Cash receipts and payments take many different forms which may include regular receipts and payments, irregular receipts and payments, capital payments and drawings/dividends.

Complete the table by inserting each example description to match the correct type of cash receipt or cash payment.

Type of receipt/payment	Example
Regular revenue receipts	
Regular revenue payments	
Exceptional receipts/payments	
Capital payments/receipts	
Drawings/dividends	

Income received from HM Customs and Revenue

Income received from the operating activities of the business which are expected to occur frequently

Income received from the operating activities of the business which are not expected to occur frequently

Income that arises from the proceeds of the sale of non-current (fixed) assets

Payments that arise from the acquisition of non-current (fixed) assets

Income received from the owner of the business

Payments made to the owner of the business

Payments due to the operating activities of the business that are expected to be incurred frequently

Payments due to the operating activities of the business that are not expected to be incurred frequently

Task 3.2

A business makes 30% of its monthly sales for cash with the remainder being sold on credit. On average 40% of the total sales are received in the month following the sale and the remainder in the second month after the sale. Sales figures are estimated to be as follows.

	£
August	240,000
September	265,000
October	280,000
November	250,000
December	220,000

What are the cash receipts from sales that are received in each of the three months from October to December?

	October £	November £	December £
Cash Sales			
October			
November			
December			
Credit sales			
August			
September			
September			
October			
October			
November			
Total cash receipts			

Task 3.3

A business purchases all of its goods on credit from suppliers. 20% of purchases are offered a discount of 2% for payment in the month of purchase and the business takes advantage of these discounts. A further 45% of purchases are paid for in the month after the purchase and the remainder are paid for two months after the purchase. Purchases figures are estimated to be as follows.

	£
August	180,000
September	165,000
October	190,000
November	200,000
December	220,000

What are the cash payments made to suppliers in each of the three months from October to December?

	October	November	December
	£	£	£

Task 3.4

(a) A business makes all of its sales on credit with a 3% settlement discount offered for payment within the month of the sale. 25% of sales take up this settlement discount and 70% of sales are paid in the following month. The remainder are bad debts.

Sales figures are as follows.

	£
March	650,000
April	600,000
May	580,000
June	550,000

What are the cash receipts from sales that are received in each of the three months from April to June?

	April £	May £	June £

Task 3.4

(b) The business is considering the effect of increasing the settlement discount to 5%. As a result, with effect from March sales, 30% of customers are expected to take the discount and all remaining customers to pay in the following month, with no bad debts.

What are the revised cash receipts from sales?

	April	May	June

Chapter 4

Task 4.1

Given below are the daily takings in a shop that is open five days a week, Monday to Friday.

	Mon	Tues	Wed	Thurs	Fri
	£	£	£	£	£
Week 1	1,260	1,600	1,630	1,780	1,830
Week 2	1,340	1,750	1,640	1,850	1,980
Week 3	1,550	1,660	1,620	1,870	1,970

Calculate the five-day moving average for the daily takings.

Week	Day	Takings	Five-day moving average
		£	£

Task 4.2

In time series analysis there are a number of elements of a time series.

Match each element of a time series analysis listed on the left with its correct description from the list on the right.

| Random variation |

Variations in the time series due to the seasonality of the business

| Trend |

Long-term variations caused by general economic factors

| Cyclical variation |

Other variations not due to the trend, cyclical or seasonal variations

| Seasonal variation |

General movement in the time series figure

Task 4.3

A company is trying to estimate its sales volumes for the first three months of next year. This is to be done by calculating a trend using the actual monthly sales volumes for the current year and a 3-point moving average.

(a) **Complete the table below to calculate the monthly sales volume trend and identify any monthly variations.**

	Sales volume	Trend	Monthly variation (volume less trend)
	Units	Units	Units
January	20,000		
February	17,400		
March	16,300		
April	22,400		
May	19,800		
June	18,700		
July	24,800		
August	22,200		
September	21,100		
October	27,200		
November	24,600		
December	23,500		

The monthly sales volume trend is [   ] units

(b) **Using the trend and the monthly variations identified in part (a) complete the table below for forecast sales volume for January, February and March of the next financial year.**

	Forecast trend	Variation	Forecast sales volume
	Units	Units	Units
January			
February			
March			

Task 4.4

Trend values for sales of barbecues by Hothouse Ltd over the last three years have been as follows:

Year	1st quarter	2nd quarter	3rd quarter	4th quarter
1	7,494	7,665	7,890	8,123
2	8,295	8,493	8,701	8,887
3	9,090	9,296	9,501	9,705

Average seasonal variations for the four quarters have been:

Quarter 1 + 53
Quarter 2 + 997
Quarter 3 + 1,203
Quarter 4 − 2,253

Use the trend and estimates of seasonal variations to forecast sales in each quarter of next year and the associated revenue if the selling price is expected to be £45 per barbecue.

Average increase in trend value   [   ]   units

Future trend values

Quarter 1
Quarter 2
Quarter 3
Quarter 4

Quarter	Trend forecast	Average seasonal variation	Forecast of actual sales units	Forecast revenue £
1				
2				
3				
4				

Task 4.5

A business currently sells its product for £30 but it is anticipated that there will be a price increase of 4% from 1 February. The sales quantities are expected to be as follows:

January	21,000 units
February	22,000 units
March	22,800 units

All sales are on credit and 40% of cash is received in the month following the sale and the remainder two months after the sale.

What are the receipts from sales that are received in March?

	£
January sales	
February sales	
Total March receipts	

Task 4.6

A business has production overheads of £347,000 in December 20X8 but it is anticipated that these will increase by 1.25% per month for the next few months. Overheads are paid the month after they are incurred.

What is the cash outflow for overheads that is paid during the month of March 20X9?

A   £347,000
B   £355,729
C   £351,338
D   £360,176

Task 4.7

A business makes purchases of a raw material which has a cost of £2.60 per kg in November 20X8. The actual and estimated price index for this material is as follows:

	Price index
November (actual)	166.3
December (estimate)	169.0
January (estimate)	173.4
February (estimate)	177.2

What is the expected price per kg (to the nearest penny) of the raw material in each of the months of December, January and February?

	£
December	
January	
February	

Chapter 5

Task 5.1

A manufacturing company is preparing its cash budget for the three months ending 31 July. The production budget is estimated to be as follows.

	April	May	June	July	August
Production quantity	1,020	1,220	1,320	1,520	1,620

The materials required for the product are 2 kg per unit costing £40 per kg and are purchased in the month prior to production and paid for in the following month. At 1 April there are 550 kgs of raw material in stock but these are to be reduced by 50 kgs per month for each of the next four months.

(a) **The purchases budget in kgs and £s for April to July**

	April	May	June	July
	Kgs	kgs	kgs	Kgs
Materials required for production				
April				
May				
June				
July				
Opening inventory (stock)				
Closing inventory (stock)				
Purchases in kgs				

	April	May	June	July
	£	£	£	£
April				
May				
June				
July				

(b) **The cash payments to suppliers for May to July**

	May	June	July
	£	£	£
Cash payments			

Task 5.2

A business manufactures and sells a single product, each unit of which requires 20 minutes of labour. The wage rate is £8.40 per hour. The production budget is anticipated to be:

	April	May	June	July
Production in units	7,200	7,050	6,450	6,000

The product is produced one month prior to sale and wages are paid in the month of production.

Calculate the cash payments for wages for each of the three months from April to June.

Labour budget – hours	April	May	June
	Hours	Hours	Hours
April			
May			
June			
Labour budget - £	April	May	June
	£	£	£
April			
May			
June			

Task 5.3

A business is about to prepare a cash budget for the quarter ending 30 September. The recent actual and estimated sales figures are as follows.

	£
April (actual)	420,000
May (actual)	400,000
June (estimate)	480,000
July (estimate)	500,000
August (estimate)	520,000
September (estimate)	510,000

All sales are on credit and the payment pattern is as follows.

20% pay in the month of sale after taking a 4% settlement discount

40% pay in the month following the sale

25% pay two months after the month of sale

12% pay three months after the month of sale

There are expected to be 3% bad debts.

(a) **Complete the table below to show the cash receipts from customers**.

		July	August	September
		£	£	£
April sales				
May sales				
June sales				
July sales				
August sales				
September sales				
Total receipts				

The purchases of the business are all on credit and it is estimated that the following purchases will be made.

	£
May	250,000
June	240,000
July	280,000
August	300,000
September	310,000

40% of purchases are paid for in the month after the purchase has been made and the remainder are paid for two months after the month of purchase.

(b) **Complete the table below to show the cash payments to suppliers.**

		July	August	September
		£	£	£
May purchases				
June purchases				
July purchases				
August purchases				
Total payments				

General overheads are anticipated to be a monthly £50,000 for June and July increasing to £55,000 thereafter. 75% of the general overheads are paid in the month in which they are incurred and the remainder in the following month. The general overheads figure includes a depreciation charge of £6,000 each month.

(c) **Complete the table below to show the cash payments for general overheads.**

		July	August	September
		£	£	£
June overheads				
July overheads				
August overheads				
September overheads				
Total overhead payments				

Additional information

- Wages are expected to be £60,000 each month and are paid in the month in which they are incurred.

- Selling expenses are expected to be 10% of the monthly sales value and are paid for in the month following the sale.

- The business has planned to purchase new equipment for £42,000 in August and in the same month to dispose of old equipment with estimated sales proceeds of £7,500.

- Overdraft interest is charged at 1% per month based on the overdraft balance at the start of the month. At 1 July it is anticipated that the business will have an overdraft of £82,000.

(d) **Referring to your answers in parts (a), (b) and (c) and the additional information above, prepare a monthly cash budget for the three months ending September.** Cash inflows should be entered as positive figures and cash outflows as negative figures. Zeros must be entered where appropriate to achieve full marks.

	July	August	September
	£	£	£
Receipts			
Receipts from credit sales			
Proceeds from sale of equipment			
Total receipts			
Payments			
Payments to suppliers			
Wages			
Overheads			
Selling expenses			
Equipment			
Overdraft interest			
Total payments			
Net cash flow			
Opening balance			
Closing balance			

Task 5.4

A manufacturing business is to prepare its cash budget for the three months ending 31 December. The business manufactures a single product which requires 3 kg of raw material per unit and 3 hours of labour per unit. Production is in the month of sale. The raw material cost is anticipated to be £9 per kg and the labour force is paid at a rate of £7.20 per hour. Each unit of the product sells for £75.

The forecast sales in units are as follows:

	August	September	October	November	December
Forecast sales – units	5,000	5,100	5,400	5,800	6,000

Sales are on credit with 40% of customers paying the month after sale and the remainder two months after the sale.

(a) **Complete the table below to calculate the timing of receipts from credit customers to be included in the cash budget.**

		October	November	December
		£	£	£
August sales				
September sales				
October sales				
November sales				
Total cash receipts				

The raw materials required for production are purchased in the month prior to production and 60% are paid for in the following month and the remainder two months after purchase. The anticipated inventory (stock) of raw materials are 3,000 kgs until the end of September and the planned inventory (stock) levels at the end of each month thereafter are as follows:

October   3,200 kgs
November   3,500 kgs
December   4,000 kgs

The production budget is as follows:	Aug	Sept	Oct	Nov	Dec
	Units	Units	Units	Units	Units
Production	5,000	5,100	5,500	5,900	6,100

(b) **Complete the following table to give the purchases budget for August to November in both kgs and £.**

	Aug	Sept	Oct	Nov
	kg	kg	kg	Kg
Kgs required for production				
Opening inventory (stock)				
Closing inventory (stock)				
Purchases in kgs				
	£	£	£	£
Purchases in £				

(c) **Using the information from part (b) and above complete the following table to calculate the payments to suppliers for October to December.**

		Oct	Nov	Dec
		£	£	£
August purchases				
September purchases				
October purchases				
November purchases				
Total cash payments				

Wages are paid in the month in which they are incurred.

(d) **Complete the table below to show the labour budget for October to December in hours and in £.**

	Oct	Nov	Dec
	Hours	Hours	Hours
Production times hours per unit			
	£	£	£
Production hours times wage rate			

Additional information

- Production overheads are expected to be £60,000 each month and are paid for in the month in which they are incurred. This figure includes depreciation of £10,000 per month for machinery.

- General overheads are anticipated to be £72,000 each month in October and November increasing to £80,000 in December and are paid in the month in which they are incurred. The figure for general overheads includes £12,000 of depreciation each month.

- The cash balance at 1 October is expected to be £40,000 in credit.

(e) **Referring to your answers in parts (a) to (d) and the additional information above, prepare a monthly cash budget for the three months ending December. Cash inflows should be entered as positive figures and cash outflows as negative figures. Zeroes must be entered where appropriate to achieve full marks.**

	October	November	December
	£	£	£
Receipts			
From credit customers			
Payments			
To credit suppliers			
Wages			
Production overheads			
General overheads			
Total payments			
Net cash flow			
Opening bank balance			
Closing bank balance			

Task 5.5

A business currently pays its suppliers with the following pattern:

60% one month after the date of purchase

40% two months after the date of purchase

On 30% of these purchases a 3% discount is offered for payment during the month of purchase but in the past the business has not taken advantage of this. If it did take advantage then 30% of purchases would be paid for in the month of purchase, 40% in the month following purchase and 30% two months after the date of purchase.

Purchases are estimated to be as follows:

	£
August	520,000
September	550,000
October	560,000
November	580,000
December	600,000

(a) **Using the table below calculate the payments to suppliers in October, November and December in accordance with the current situation where no settlement discounts are taken.**

	October	November	December
	£	£	£
August purchases			
September purchases			
October purchases			
November purchases			
Total cash payments			

(b) **Using the table below calculate the payments made to suppliers in October, November and December in accordance with the new settlement discount scheme described above on the assumption that the scheme begins in October.**

	October	November	December
	£	£	£
August purchases			
September purchases			
October purchases			
November purchases			
December purchases			
Total cash payments			

Task 5.6

(a) At 31 March a business had receivables (debtors) of £260,000. Planned sales for the following three months in units are:

April	140,000 units
May	150,000 units
June	155,000 units

All sales are made on credit. On average 40% of receivables (debtors) pay during the month after the sale and the remainder pay two months after the date of sale.

The receivables (debtors) at 31 March can be assumed to pay as follows:

	£
In April	140,000
In May	120,000
	260,000

Sales are made at a price of £1.00 per unit.

However, in the light of current economic circumstances it is being anticipated that the sales price will have to be reduced to £0.90 per unit.

Use the table below to calculate the effect of the changes in the forecast amounts for April, May and June.

	April £	May £	June £
Original value of forecast sales			
Original timing of receipts			
Revised value of forecast sales			
Revised timing of receipts			
Increase/(decrease) in sales receipts			

Task 5.6

(b)   An extract from the original cash budget is set out below.

	April	May	June
	£	£	£
Net cash flow	(12,000)	40,000	44,000
Opening bank balance	(20,000)	(32,000)	8,000
Closing bank balance	(32,000)	8,000	52,000

Using your calculation of the revised receipts in (a) above, complete the table to show the impact of the change in the forecast amounts on the budgeted bank balances.

	April	May	June
	£	£	£
Original net cash flow	(12,000)	40,000	44,000
Increase/(decrease) in sales receipts per (a)			
Revised net cash flow			
Opening bank balance			
Closing bank balance			

Chapter 6

Task 6.1

Are the following statements True or False? Tick the correct box.

Primary banks are those that are involved with the cheque clearing system.

True

False

Secondary banks are also known as commercial banks.

True

False

Task 6.2

What are the four main benefits of financial intermediation?

-
-
-
-

Task 6.3

A bank customer has an overdraft.

Which party is the trade payable (creditor)? Tick as appropriate.

Bank

Customer

Task 6.4

State six of a bank's main duties to its customer.

-
-
-
-
-
-

Task 6.5

Pravina, an eighteen-year old who lives next door to you, is about to open her first bank account.

Explain to her the rights the bank has in its relationship with her.

....

Task 6.6

What are the most common reasons underlying a business's identification of a future cash deficit or the need to raise additional finance?

....

Task 6.7

Which of the following best describe the main features of overdraft finance?

(i)   High interest rate
(ii)   Repayable in instalments
(iii)   Useful for capital expenditure
(iv)   Low interest rate
(v)   Short-term form of finance
(vi)   Repayable on demand
(vii) Available as long as required

A   (i), (ii), (iii)
B   (i), (v), (vi)
C   (iii), (iv), (vii)
D   (ii), (iv), (v)

....

Task 6.8

Which of the following best describes the main features of a bank loan?

(i)   High interest rate
(ii)   Repayments can be negotiated
(iii)   Useful for capital expenditure
(iv)   Low interest rate
(v)   Short-term form of finance
(vi)   Repayable on demand
(vii) Available as long as required

A   (i), (ii), (iii)
B   (ii), (iv), (vi)
C   (i), (v), (vii)
D   (ii), (iii), (iv)

....

Task 6.9

Both overdraft finance and bank loan finance have various advantages.

Complete the table by entering each of the advantages against the correct type of financing.

Type of finance	Advantages
Overdraft	
Bank loan	

Relatively low cost
Useful to fund capital expenditure
Precise amount required does not need to be known
Security not normally required
Covenants not normally included
Repayments can be negotiated

....

Task 6.10

An agricultural business has purchased a new tractor costing £63,800. It has funded the purchase with a medium-term bank loan for the full amount. The business must repay the loan over three years, with monthly payments of £2,380.

Assuming simple interest, calculate the total interest cost and the simple annual interest rate.

....

Task 6.11

A business has applied for a bank loan of £22,500 to purchase some new computers for its head office. The bank requires the loan to be paid off in equal monthly instalments over two and a half years, charging simple interest at 5.25% per annum on the initial loan capital.

What are the monthly payments for the repayments of the capital and the interest on this loan?

....

Task 6.12

A small private limited company requires finance for an expansion project which will require £50,000 of capital expenditure and £10,000 of additional working capital. The finance director has been investigating methods of raising this finance and has found three potential options.

Option 1   A bank loan for £60,000 secured on the non-current (fixed) assets of the company. The loan is to be repayed in equal instalments over a three-year period and has a fixed rate of interest for the first year of 5%. Thereafter the rate of interest will be variable at 2.5% above the base rate. There will be an arrangement fee for the loan of 0.6% of the bank loan payable at the start of the loan term.

Option 2   The four family directors will all take out a personal secured loan of £15,000 at an annual interest rate of 4%. This money will then be loaned to the company and the personal interest cost for the directors recouped from the company.

Option 3   A bank loan for £50,000 could be taken out secured on the value of the new machinery required for the expansion. The loan will be repaid in equal instalments over five years and the interest is at a fixed rate of 5.5% based upon the outstanding capital balance at the start of the year. An arrangement fee of 0.75% of the bank loan is payable at the beginning of the loan term.

In order to fund the working capital the bank is also offering an overdraft facility of £15,000 which attracts an annual interest rate of 11%. The directors believe that they will require an average overdraft of £8,500 for just the first ten months of the year.

The Articles of Association of the company include the following in respect of the raising of finance:

- Loan finance can be secured on the assets of the company.

- The company must not accept loans from officers or directors of the company.

- The maximum overdraft allowed is £18,000.

- The interest cost to the company of any financing options should be kept as low as possible.

(a) **Complete the table below to calculate the cost to the company for the first year of financing under each of the three options.**

	Arrangement fee	Loan interest £	Overdraft interest £	Total cost £
Option 1				
Option 2				
Option 3				

(b) **Which financial option should the company select taking account of the provisions of the Articles of Association?**

Option 1	
Option 2	
Option 3	
None of the options	

Chapter 7

Task 7.1

Briefly explain the three main general factors that should influence any decisions regarding investment of surplus funds.

Task 7.2

Which of the following are true about gilt-edged securities?

(i)   They are issued by local authorities.
(ii)   They are variable rate investments.
(iii)   The interest is paid twice a year.
(iv)   They are fixed rate investments.
(v)   They are issued by the government.

A   (i), (ii), (iii)
B   (ii), (iii), (v)
C   (iii), (iv), (v)
D   (ii), (iv), (v)

Task 7.3

Interest rates are set to fall in the near future.

What effect will this have on the price of gilt-edged securities? Tick the correct answer.

Their price will rise.

Their price will fall.

Task 7.4

A business has £100,000 to invest for a period of approximately six months. Investment in either a bank deposit account or gilt-edged securities is being considered.

What would be the effect of an increase in interest rates on both of these potential investments? Tick the appropriate boxes in the table below.

	Bank deposit	Gilt-edged securities
Increase in value		
Decrease in value		
No effect		

Task 7.5

A business makes a proportion of its sales for cash through a factory outlet.

What security procedures should be adopted for the safe custody of this cash?

....

Task 7.6

Azrina Ltd manufactures cycles. The company's long-term cash flow forecasts suggests a cash surplus of £1 million will be generated in 20X7 and £1.75 million in 20X8.

The company is considering its future cash management strategy and is examining four business strategies.

For each of the following four strategy scenarios, complete the table to show what action you would take to manage the cash surplus.

(a) No further growth in Azrina Ltd's existing business and no plans for further capital investment

(b) Plans for an acquisition of a cycle parts manufacturer (valued up to £5 million) when a suitable opportunity arises

(c) Development in 20X7 and 20X8 of several new product lines requiring capital investment of £2.5 million

(d) Phased development of two new product lines requiring capital investment of £1.25 million and the intention to acquire another cycle parts manufacturer (value up to £3 million) when a suitable opportunity arises

Possible action	Strategy
Invest in marketable securities	
Spend surplus cash	
Repay surplus cash to owners	
Retain cash for ease of availability	

....

Task 7.7

A company has produced a cash budget and believes that it will have £50,000 to invest in three months' time. The finance director has identified three possible investment options:

Option 1   Maximum investment £75,000, minimum investment £15,000. Interest rate 1.8% above base rate. 60-day notice period. Low risk and no investment in shares.

Option 2   Minimum investment of £50,000. Interest rate of 2.5%. 90-day notice period. Medium risk and no investment in shares.

Option 3   Minimum investment of £55,000. Interest rate of 3%. 30-day notice period. Low risk and no investment in shares.

The company's treasury policy for investment is as follows:

■   Interest rate must be at least 2% above base rate which is currently 0.4%.
■   The investment must be convertible into cash within 60 days.
■   The investment must be low or medium risk.
■   The investment must not include shares.

(a)   **Complete the table below to show which of the policy requirements are met by each of the options.**

	Investment of £50,000	Interest 2% above base rate	Convertible within 60 days	Low/medium risk	No shares
Option 1					
Option 2					
Option 3					

(b)   **Which option should be selected?**

Option 1	
Option 2	
Option 3	
None of the options	

Chapter 8

Task 8.1

Given below is the cash budget for the month of June for a business together with the actual cash flows for the month of June.

Cash budget June

	Budget £	Actual £
Receipts:		
Cash sales receipts	101,000	94,000
Credit sales receipts	487,000	475,000
Total receipts	588,000	569,000
Payments:		
Credit suppliers	(303,000)	(294,000)
Wages	(155,000)	(162,000)
Variable overheads	(98,600)	(99,400)
Fixed overheads	(40,000)	(40,000)
Capital expenditure	–	(45,000)
Total payments	(596,600)	(640,400)
Net cash flow for the month	(8,600)	(71,400)
Bank b/f	20,300	20,300
Bank c/f	11,700	(51,100)

Complete the table below to compare the actual cash flows to the budgeted cash flows and identify any variances indicating whether they are favourable or adverse variances.

	Budget £	Actual £	Variance £	Adv/Fav £
Receipts:				
Cash sales receipts				
Credit sales receipts				
Total receipts				
Payments:				
Credit suppliers				

	Budget	Actual	Variance	Adv/Fav
	£	£	£	£
Wages				
Variable overheads				
Fixed overheads				
Capital expenditure				
Total payments				
Net cash flow				
Balance b/f				
Balance c/f				

Task 8.2

Given below is the cash budget and actual cash flows for a business for the month of July.

	Budget £	Actual £
Receipts:		
Cash sales	264,000	277,000
Receipts from credit customers	888,000	863,000
Proceeds from sale of non-current (fixed) assets	–	22,000
Total receipts	1,152,000	1,162,000
Payments:		
Payments to credit suppliers	742,000	777,000
Wages	197,000	197,000
Variable overheads	51,300	58,700
Fixed overheads	66,000	68,000
Purchase of non-current (fixed) assets	–	46,000
Dividend payment	50,000	50,000
Total payments	1,106,300	1,196,700
Net cash flow	45,700	(34,700)
Opening cash balance	16,200	16,200
Closing cash balance	61,900	(18,500)

(a) **Reconcile the budgeted cash balance at 31 July to the actual cash balance at that date using the table below. Select the appropriate description for each entry.**

	£
Budgeted closing bank balance	
Surplus/shortfall in cash sales	
Surplus/shortfall in credit sales receipts	
Increase/decrease in proceeds from sales from non-current (fixed) assets	
Increase/decrease/no change in payments to credit suppliers	
Increase/decrease in wages	
Increase/decrease in variable overheads	
	£
Increase/decrease in fixed overheads	
Increase/decrease in purchase of non-current (fixed) assets	
Increase/decrease/no change in dividend payments	
Actual closing bank balance	

(b) **What actions could have been taken to avoid the use of overdraft finance by the end of the month?**

    A   Delay capital expenditure
    B   Chase customers to pay sooner
    C   Delay payments to suppliers
    D   Marketing campaign to increase sales

Task 8.3

(a) **A business is in the process of comparing its budgeted and actual cash flows for February. Complete the table below to identify any variances indicating whether they are favourable (+) or adverse (-) variances.**

	Budget February	Actual February	Variance
	£	£	£
Cash receipts			
Receipts from sales	148,800	145,600	
Deposit account interest	100	100	
Total cash receipts	148,900	145,700	
Cash payments			
Payments to suppliers	−41,600	−56,000	
Salaries	−43,000	−45,150	
Administration overheads	−30,000	−30,000	
Capital expenditure	−20,000	−6,000	
Total payments	−134,600	−137,150	
Net cash flow	14,300	8,550	
Opening cash balance	−25,900	−25,900	
Closing cash balance	−11,600	−17,350	

(b) **Reconcile the budgeted cash balance at end February to the actual cash balance at that date using the table below. Select the appropriate description for each entry.**

	£
Budgeted closing bank balance	
Surplus/shortfall in sales receipts	
Surplus/shortfall/no change in deposit account interest	
Increase/decrease in payments to credit suppliers	
Increase/decrease in salaries	
Increase/decrease/no change in administration overheads	
Increase/decrease in capital expenditure	
Actual closing bank balance	

(c) **From the list below, choose the appropriate explanations for the variances identified.**

Sales receipts	

Payments to suppliers	

Salaries	

Capital expenditure	

Explanations
Increase product selling price
Cut back on overtime working
Negotiated credit with supplier of equipment, provided initial deposit paid in month of purchase
Issued less share capital
Loss of customers
Used up material from stock
Bonus paid to staff
Increase in suppliers prices

Task 8.4

Variances between actual cash flows and budgeted cash flows can be due to a variety of reasons. There are also a number of courses of action which are available to minimise the effect of adverse variances and to capitalise on the benefit of favourable variances.

Match each variance listed on the left with a possible course of action from the list on the right.

Adverse wages cost variance

Continue to take supplier discounts

Adverse credit sales receipts variance

Schedule less overtime

Favourable credit supplier payments variance

Delay capital expenditure

Adverse capital expenditure variance

Offer settlement discounts for early payment

Answer bank

Answer bank

Cash Management Answer Bank

Chapter 1

Task 1.1

The cash operating cycle time is the <u>inventory (stock) turnover period plus receivables' (debtors') payment period less payables' (creditors') payment period</u>.

Liquid assets include <u>cash and short-term investments</u>.

....

Task 1.2

C   87 days

Cash operating cycle:

	Days
Inventory (stock) turnover 250/1,800 × 365	51
Receivables' (debtors') turnover 550/2,600 × 365	77
	128
Less: payables' (creditors') turnover 200/1,800 × 365	(41)
Cash operating cycle	87

....

Task 1.3

D   4 months

	Months
Raw material turnover period	4.0
Less: credit taken from suppliers	(3.0)
Finished goods inventory (stock) turnover period	1.0
Receivables' (debtors') payment period	2.0
Cash operating cycle	4.0

....

Task 1.4

B

Offering an early settlement discount to customers will hopefully encourage customers to pay earlier. This will have the effect of reducing the receivables' (debtors') collection period, which will in turn reduce the cash operating cycle of the business.

Task 1.5

	Before	After
Inventory (stock) turnover	45	54
Receivables' (debtors') collection period	40	46
Payables' (creditors') payment period	60	60
Cash operating cycle	45 + 40 – 60 = 25	54 + 46 – 60 = 40

Task 1.6

Over-trading occurs when a business has <u>too little</u> working capital.

Over-capitalisation occurs when a business has <u>too much</u> working capital.

Chapter 2

Task 2.1

If a business makes a profit this means that <u>its revenue is greater than its expenses</u>.

Cash flow and profit will <u>not normally</u> be the same figure for a period.

Task 2.2

1   Accruals accounting

2   Non-cash expenses

3   Capital introduced or dividends/drawings paid

4   Purchase of non-current (fixed) assets

5   Sale of non-current (fixed) assets

Task 2.3

	£'000
Sales receipts	820
Purchase payments	575
Overhead payments	95

Workings

Sales receipts	=	860 + 45 – 85	=	820
Purchase payments	=	600 + 75 – 100	=	575
Overhead payments	=	100 + 40 – 45	=	95

Task 2.4

D   £39,500

The NBV of non-current (fixed) assets increased by £27,000 but this was after deducting £12,500 of depreciation, so the cash paid for new assets must have been £27,000 + £12,500 = £39,500.

Task 2.5

B   £1,960 loss

The net book value of the machine at the date of disposal is £25,760 (64,400-38,640). If it is sold for £23,800, it must have been sold at a loss of £1,960 (23,800-25,760).

···

Task 2.6

D   £91,500

The net book value of the building at the date of disposal is £56,500 (105,000-48,500). If it is sold for a profit of £35,000, it must have been sold for more than its net book value, so the cash proceeds are £56,500+£35000 = £91,500.

···

Chapter 3

Task 3.1

Type of receipt/payment	Example
Regular revenue receipts	Income received from the operating activities of the business which are expected to occur frequently
Regular revenue payments	Payments due to the operating activities of the business that are expected to be incurred frequently
Exceptional receipts/payments	Income received from HM Customs and Revenue
	Income received from the operating activities of the business which are not expected to occur frequently
	Payments due to the operating activities of the business that are not expected to be incurred frequently
Capital payments/receipts	Income that arises from the proceeds of the sale of non-current (fixed) assets
	Payments that arise from the acquisition of non-current (fixed) assets
	Income received from the owner of the business
Drawings/dividends	Payments made to the owner of the business

Task 3.2

	October £	November £	December £
Cash sales			
October 280,000 × 30%	84,000		
November 250,000 × 30%		75,000	
December 220,000 × 30%			66,000
Credit sales			
August 240,000 × 30%	72,000		
September 265,000 × 40%	106,000		
September 265,000 × 30%		79,500	
October 280,000 × 40%		112,000	
October 280,000 × 30%			84,000
November 250,000 × 40%			100,000
Total cash receipts	**262,000**	**266,500**	**250,000**

Task 3.3

	October £	November £	December £
August 180,000 × 35%	63,000		
September 165,000 × 45%	74,250		
September 165,000 × 35%		57,750	
October 190,000 × 20% × 98%	37,240		
October 190,000 × 45%		85,500	
October 190,000 × 35%			66,500
November 200,000 × 20% × 98%		39,200	
November 200,000 × 45%			90,000
December 220,000 × 20% × 98%			43,120
Total cash payments	**174,490**	**182,450**	**199,620**

Task 3.4

(a)

	April £	May £	June £
March sales 650,000 × 70%	455,000		
April sales 600,000 × 25% × 97%	145,500		
April sales 600,000 × 70%		420,000	
May sales 580,000 × 25% × 97%		140,650	
May sales 580,000 × 70%			406,000
June sales 550,000 × 25% × 97%			133,375
Total cash receipts	**600,500**	**560,650**	**539,375**

Task 3.4

(b)

	April £	May £	June £
March sales 650,000 × 70%	455,000		
April sales 600,000 × 30% × 95%	171,000		
April sales 600,000 × 70%		420,000	
May sales 580,000 × 30% × 95%		165,300	
May sales 580,000 × 70%			406,000
June sales 550,000 × 30% × 95%			156,750
Total cash receipts	**626,000**	**585,300**	**562,750**

Chapter 4

Task 4.1

Week	Day	Takings £	Five-day moving average £
1	Monday	1,260	
	Tuesday	1,600	
	Wednesday	1,630	1,620
	Thursday	1,780	1,636
	Friday	1,830	1,666
2	Monday	1,340	1,668
	Tuesday	1,750	1,682
	Wednesday	1,640	1,712
	Thursday	1,850	1,754
	Friday	1,980	1,736
3	Monday	1,550	1,732
	Tuesday	1,660	1,736
	Wednesday	1,620	1,734
	Thursday	1,870	
	Friday	1,970	

Task 4.2

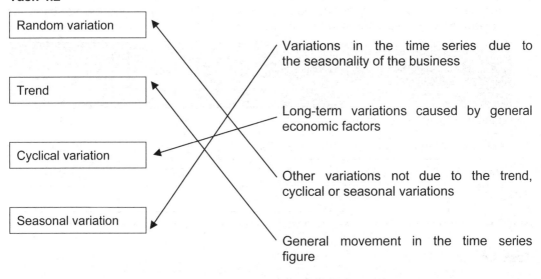

Random variation

Variations in the time series due to the seasonality of the business

Trend

Long-term variations caused by general economic factors

Cyclical variation

Other variations not due to the trend, cyclical or seasonal variations

Seasonal variation

General movement in the time series figure

Task 4.3

(a)

	Sales volume	Trend	Monthly variation (volume less trend)
	Units	Units	Units
January	20,000		
February	17,400	17,900	−500
March	16,300	18,700	−2,400
April	22,400	19,500	2,900
May	19,800	20,300	−500
June	18,700	21,100	−2,400
July	24,800	21,900	2,900
August	22,200	22,700	−500
September	21,100	23,500	−2,400
October	27,200	24,300	2,900
November	24,600	25,100	−500
December	23,500		

The monthly sales volume trend is 800 units.

calculated as ((25,100 − 17,900)/9 changes in trend)

(b) The variation for January is not given. However the variations can be seen to repeat and sum to zero on a quarterly basis (-500, -2400, +2900). Thus the variation for December would be -2400 and that for January +2900.

	Forecast trend	Variation	Forecast sales volume
	Units	Units	Units
January (25,100 + (2 × 800))	26,700	2,900	29,600
February (25,100 + (3 × 800))	27,500	−500	27,000
March (25,100 + (4 × 800))	28,300	−2,400	25,900

Task 4.4

$$\text{Average increase in trend value} = \frac{(9,705 - 7,494)}{11}$$

$$= 201 \text{ units}$$

Future trend values

Quarter 1 (9,705 + 201) 9,906 units
Quarter 2 (9,705 + (2 × 201)) 10,107 units
Quarter 3 (9,705 + (3 × 201)) 10,308 units
Quarter 4 (9,705 + (4 × 201)) 10,509 units

Quarter	Trend forecast	Average seasonal variation	Forecast of actual sales units	Forecast revenue £
1	9,906	+53	9,959	448,155
2	10,107	+997	11,104	499,680
3	10,308	+1,203	11,511	517,995
4	10,509	−2,253	8,256	371,520

Task 4.5

	£
January sales 21,000 × £30 × 60%	378,000
February sales 22,000 × £30 × 1.04 × 40%	274,560
Total March receipts	**652,560**

Task 4.6   B

March cash outflow for overheads   = £347,000 × 1.0125 × 1.0125

= £355,729

....

Task 4.7

	£
December	2.60 × 169.0/166.3 = £2.64
January	2.60 × 173.4/166.3 = £2.71
February	2.60 × 177.2/166.3 = £2.77

....

Chapter 5

Task 5.1

(a) Purchases budget

	April	May	June	July
	kgs	kgs	kgs	kgs
Materials required for production				
April 1,220 × 2 kg	2,440			
May 1,320 × 2 kg		2,640		
June 1,520 × 2 kg			3,040	
July 1,620 × 2 kg				3,240
Opening inventory (stock)	(550)	(500)	(450)	(400)
Closing inventory (stock)	500	450	400	350
Purchases in kgs	2,390	2,590	2,990	3,190

	April	May	June	July
	£	£	£	£
April 2,390 × £40	95,600			
May 2,590 × £40		103,600		
June 2,990 × £40			119,600	
July 3,190 × £40				127,600

(b) Cash payments to suppliers for May to July

	May	June	July
	£	£	£
Cash payments	95,600	103,600	119,600

Task 5.2

Labour budget – hours	April	May	June
	Hours	Hours	Hours
April 7,050/3	2,350		
May 6,450/3		2,150	
June 6,000/3			2,000
Labour budget - £	April	May	June
	£	£	£
April 2,350 × £8.40	19,740		
May 2,150 × £8.40		18,060	
June 2,000 × £8.40			16,800

Task 5.3

(a) **Cash receipts from customers**

		July	August	September
		£	£	£
April sales	420,000 × 12%	50,400		
May sales	400,000 × 25%	100,000		
	400,000 × 12%		48,000	
June sales	480,000 × 40%	192,000		
	480,000 × 25%		120,000	
	480,000 × 12%			57,600
July sales	500,000 × 20% × 96%	96,000		
	500,000 × 40%		200,000	
	500,000 × 25%			125,000
August sales	520,000 × 20% × 96%		99,840	
	520,000 × 40%			208,000
September sales	510,000 × 20% × 96%			97,920
Total receipts		**438,400**	**467,840**	**488,520**

(b) **Cash payments to suppliers**

		July	August	September
		£	£	£
May purchases	250,000 × 60%	150,000		
June purchases	240,000 × 40%	96,000		
	240,000 × 60%		144,000	
July purchases	280,000 × 40%		112,000	
	280,000 × 60%			168,000
August purchases	300,000 × 40%			120,000
Total payments		**246,000**	**256,000**	**288,000**

(c) **Cash payments for general overheads**

		July	August	September
		£	£	£
June overheads	(50,000 – 6,000) × 25%	11,000		
July overheads	(50,000 – 6,000) × 75%	33,000		
	(50,000 – 6,000) × 25%		11,000	
August overheads	(55,000 – 6,000) × 75%		36,750	
	(55,000 – 6,000) × 25%			12,250
September overheads	(55,000 – 6,000) × 75%			36,750
Total overhead payments		**44,000**	**47,750**	**49,000**

(d) **Cash budget – July to September**

	July	August	September
	£	£	£
Receipts			
Receipts from credit sales	438,400	467,840	488,520
Proceeds from sale of equipment	0	7,500	0
Total receipts	**438,400**	**475,340**	**488,520**
Payments			
Payments to suppliers	–246,000	–256,000	–288,000

	July	August	September
	£	£	£
Wages	−60,000	−60,000	−60,000
Overheads	−44,000	−47,750	−49,000
Selling expenses	−48,000	−50,000	−52,000
Equipment	0	−42,000	0
Overdraft interest	−820	−424	−233
Total payments	**−398,820**	**−456,174**	**−449,233**
Net cash flow	39,580	19,166	39,287
Opening balance	−82,000	−42,420	−23,254
Closing balance	**−42,420**	**−23,254**	**16,033**

••

Task 5.4

(a) **Cash receipts from sales**

		October	November	December
		£	£	£
August sales	5,000 × £75 × 60%	225,000		
September sales	5,100 × £75 × 40%	153,000		
	5,100 × £75 × 60%		229,500	
October sales	5,400 × £75 × 40%		162,000	
	5,400 × £75 × 60%			243,000
November sales	5,800 × £75 × 40%			174,000
Total cash receipts		**378,000**	**391,500**	**417,000**

(b) Purchases budget

	Aug	Sept	Oct	Nov
	kg	kg	kg	kg
Kgs required for production Production × 3 kg	15,300	16,500	17,700	18,300
Opening inventory (stock)	(3,000)	(3,000)	(3,000)	(3,200)
Closing inventory (stock)	3,000	3,000	3,200	3,500
Purchases in kgs	**15,300**	**16,500**	**17,900**	**18,600**
	£	£	£	£
Purchases in £ Kgs × £9	**137,700**	**148,500**	**161,100**	**167,400**

(c) Payments to suppliers

		Oct	Nov	Dec
		£	£	£
August purchases	137,700 × 40%	55,080		
September purchases	148,500 × 60%	89,100		
	148,500 × 40%		59,400	
October purchases	161,100 × 60%		96,660	
	161,100 × 40%			64,440
November purchases	167,400 × 60%			100,440
Total cash payments		**144,180**	**156,060**	**164,880**

(d) Labour budget

	Oct	Nov	Dec
	Hours	Hours	Hours
Production × 3 hours	16,500	17,700	18,300
	£	£	£
Production hours × £7.20	118,800	127,440	131,760

(e) **Cash budget – October to December**

	October	November	December
	£	£	£
Receipts			
From credit customers	**378,000**	**391,500**	**417,000**
Payments			
To credit suppliers	−44,180	−156,060	−164,880
Wages	−18,800	−127,440	−131,760
Production overheads	−50,000	−50,000	−50,000
General overheads	−60,000	−60,000	−68,000
Total payments	**−372,980**	**−393,500**	**−414,640**
Net cash flow	5,020	−2,000	2,360
Opening bank balance	40,000	45,020	43,020
Closing bank balance	**45,020**	**43,020**	**45,380**

Task 5.5

(a) **Payments to suppliers with no settlement discount**

		October	November	December
		£	£	£
August purchases	520,000 × 40%	208,000		
September purchases	550,000 × 60%	330,000		
	550,000 × 40%		220,000	
October purchases	560,000 × 60%		336,000	
	560,000 × 40%			224,000
November purchases	580,000 × 60%			348,000
Total cash payments		**538,000**	**556,000**	**572,000**

(b) **Payments to suppliers with settlement discount**

		October	November	December
		£	£	£
August purchases	520,000 × 40%	208,000		
September purchases	550,000 × 60%	330,000		
	550,000 × 40%		220,000	
October purchases	560,000 × 30% × 97%	162,960		
	560,000 × 40%		224,000	
	560,000 × 30%			168,000
November purchases	580,000 × 30% × 97%		168,780	
	580,000 × 40%			232,000
December purchases	600,000 × 30% × 97%			174,600
Total cash payments		**700,960**	**612,780**	**574,600**

Task 5.6

(a)

	April	May	June
	£	£	£
Original value of forecast sales (£1 per unit)	140,000	150,000	155,000
Original timing of receipts	140,000	176,000	144,000
Revised value of forecast sales (£0.90 per unit)	126,000	135,000	139,500
Revised timing of receipts	140,000	170,400	129,600
Increase/(decrease) in sales receipts	**0**	**(5,600)**	**(14,400)**

Working

Original timing of receipts

May	120,000 + (40% × 140,000) = 176,000
June	(60% × 140,000) + (40% × 150,000) = 144,000

Revised timing of receipts

May	120,000 + (40% × 126,000) = 170,400
June	(60% × 126,000) + (40% × 135,000) = 129,600

Task 5.6

(b)

	April	May	June
	£	£	£
Original net cash flow	(12,000)	40,000	44,000
Increase/(decrease) in sales receipts per (a)	0	(5,600)	(14,400)
Revised net cash flow	(12,000)	34,400	29,600
Opening bank balance	(20,000)	(32,000)	2,400
Closing bank balance	(32,000)	2,400	32,000

Chapter 6

Task 6.1

Primary banks are those that are involved with the cheque clearing system.

True	✓
False	

Secondary banks are also known as commercial banks.

True	
False	✓

··

Task 6.2

The four main benefits of financial intermediation are:

- Small amounts deposited by savers can be combined to provide larger loan packages to businesses.
- Short-term savings can be transferred into long-term borrowings.
- Search costs are reduced as companies seeking loan finance can approach a bank directly rather than finding individuals to lend to them.
- Risk is reduced as an individual's savings are not tied up with one individual borrower directly.

··

Task 6.3

Bank	
Customer	✓

··

Task 6.4

A bank's main duties to its customers are:

- It must honour a customer's cheque provided that it is correctly made out, there is no legal reason for not honouring it and the customer has enough funds or overdraft limit to cover the amount of the cheque.
- The bank must credit cash/cheques that are paid into the customer's account.
- If the customer makes a written request for repayment of funds in their account, for example by writing a cheque, the bank must repay the amount on demand.
- The bank must comply with the customer's instructions given by direct debit mandate or standing order.
- The bank must provide a statement showing the transactions on the account within a reasonable period and provide details of the balance on the customer's account.

- The bank must respect the confidentiality of the customer's affairs unless the bank is required by law, public duty or its own interest to disclose details or where the customer gives their consent for such disclosure.

- The bank must tell the customer if there has been an attempt to forge the customer's signature on a cheque.

- The bank should use care and skill in its actions.

- The bank must provide reasonable notice if it is to close a customer's account.

Note: only six points were required.

Task 6.5

Use of money

You cannot restrict the ways in which the bank uses your money; the money can be used in any ways that are **legally and morally acceptable**. However, the bank must make the money available to you according to the terms of your deposit; if you are opening a current account it must be **available on demand**.

Overdrawn balances

If your account shows a negative or debit balance (an **overdraft**), the bank has the right to be repaid this balance on demand. The only exception is if the bank has granted you an **overdraft facility**, which requires the bank to give you a period of notice if it wishes you to pay back what you owe it.

Charges and commissions

The bank can charge you **interest** on overdrawn balances, and can also levy **other charges and commissions** for use of its services. Depending on the terms of your account, this can even include charges for drawing cheques from your account, and withdrawing money from cashpoint machines.

Duty of care

You owe the bank a duty of care, particularly when **drawing cheques**. You should not issue cheques that are signed but lack other details such as payee or amount, nor should you write cheques out in pencil as they can easily be altered.

You should also **take care of cards** that the bank issues to you (credit, debit and cashpoint cards) and keep your **PIN number** (the number that you need to enter to use the bank's cashpoint machines) secure.

Task 6.6

The most common reasons for a business identifying a future cash deficit or the need to raise additional finance are to:

- Fund day-to-day working capital
- Increase working capital
- Reduce payables (creditors)
- Purchase non-current (fixed) assets
- Acquire another business

Task 6.7

B

....

Task 6.8

D

....

Task 6.9

Type of finance	Advantages
Overdraft	Relatively low cost Precise amount required does not need to be known Security not normally required Covenants not normally included
Bank loan	Useful to fund capital expenditure Repayments can be negotiated

....

Task 6.10

Total repayments will be 36 x £2,380 = £85,680.

If the business has borrowed £63,800 to buy the tractor, the total interest cost is 85,680 – 63,800 = £21,880.

Over the three years of the loan, the total interest is 21,880/63,800 = 34.3%. This is equivalent to 11.4% simple interest per annum.

....

Task 6.11

Repayment of capital = 22,500/30 = £750 per month

Repayment of interest = (22,500 x 5.25%)/12 = £98.44

....

Task 6.12

(a)

	Arrangement fee £	Loan interest £	Overdraft interest £	Total cost £
Option 1	360	3,000		3,360
Option 2		2,400		2,400
Option 3	375	2,750	779	3,904

Note: overdraft interest is calculated as £8,500 × 11% × $^{10}/_{12}$ = £779

(b)

Option 1	✓
Option 2	
Option 3	
None of the options	

Chapter 7

Task 7.1

The three main general factors that should influence any decisions regarding investment of surplus funds are:

- Risk
- Return
- Liquidity

When cash is invested there are two main risks. There is the risk that the value of the investment will fall and there is also the risk that the return from the investment will be lower than expected due to changes in market interest rates. When a business is investing surplus funds it will generally wish to invest in investments where the risk of loss is fairly minimal.

The return on an investment has two potential aspects, the income return and the capital return. Most investments will pay some form of interest or dividend which is the income return. However, most investments will also tend to fluctuate in value over time and this is the capital return (or capital loss). In general, the higher the risk of an investment the higher will be the expected rate of return and *vice versa*.

Liquidity is the term used for the ease and speed with which an investment can be converted into cash. Any investments which are widely traded on a market, such as the money markets, will be very liquid but investments such as a bank deposit account which requires three months' notice to withdraw the funds would not be a liquid investment. The more liquid an investment is the lower the return is likely to be as less liquid investments will pay higher returns to attract investors.

Task 7.2

C

Task 7.3

| Their price will rise. | ✓ |
| Their price will fall. | |

Task 7.4

	Bank deposit	Gilt-edged securities
Increase in value		
Decrease in value		✓
No effect	✓	

Task 7.5

Security procedures for the safe custody of cash include the following:

Physical procedures – any cash or cheques received must be kept safe at all times and must only be accessible to authorised individuals within the organisation. Therefore, cash should be kept under lock and key either in a cash box, lockable till or safe. Only authorised individuals should have access to the keys.

Checks for valid payment – payments received in cash will, of course, be valid provided that any notes are not forged. However if cheques are accepted as payment then they must be supported by a valid cheque guarantee card and be correctly drawn up, dated and signed. If debit or credit cards are accepted then basic checks should be made on the card and signature and authorisation must be sought for payments which exceed the floor limit.

Reconciliation of cash received – when payments are received in the form of cash, cheques or debit and credit cards then a list of all cash, cheque and card receipts taken during the day must be kept. This list must then be reconciled at the end of each day to the amount of cash in the till, cash box or safe. The list may be manual as each sale is made or may be automatically recorded on the till roll as each sale is rung in.

This reconciliation should not be carried out by the person responsible for making the sales but by some other responsible official. Any discrepancies between the amount of cash recorded as taken during the day and the amount physically left at the end of the day must be investigated.

Banking procedures – any cash, cheques and card vouchers should be banked as soon as possible and intact each day. This not only ensures the physical safety of the cash but also that it cannot be used by employees for unauthorised purposes. It also means that once the money is in the bank it is earning the business the maximum amount of interest. All cash should be banked as soon as possible but if it is not possible to bank it until the following day then either the cash must be left in a locked safe overnight or in the bank's overnight safe.

Recording procedures – for security purposes the paying-in slip for the bank should be made out by someone other than the person paying the money into the bank. The total on the paying-in slip should be reconciled to the till records or cash list for the day.

....

Task 7.6

Possible action	Strategy
Invest in marketable securities	(b)
Spend surplus cash	(c)
Repay surplus cash to owners	(a)
Retain cash for ease of availability	(d)

Justifications for answers

(a) No further growth/no plans for further capital expansion.

   Action. An increased or **special dividend** should be paid to shareholders; the company could also consider a **share buyback**, by means of which shares would be repurchased from the shareholders and cancelled.

Reason. If no further investments are planned, cash surplus to the needs of the business should be **returned to shareholders** so that they can use it for other investment opportunities. A small cash surplus should however be maintained.

(b) Acquisition of manufacturer

Action. Invest the cash surplus in **marketable securities** (eg Certificates of Deposit, commercial paper) or bank deposits.

Reason. Such investments ensure that the company will make a **return on its money** while retaining sufficient liquidity for when it makes an acquisition.

(c) Development of new product lines

Action. **Spend** the **cash surplus** on the proposed capital investments.

Reason. Unless there is some other possible use for the funds, eg to fund an acquisition, it will be better to use the cash surplus rather than borrowing to **fund the capital investment**, since the cost of debt finance is likely to exceed the return achievable on cash investments.

(d) Acquisition of manufacturer and development of product lines

Action. **Retain the cash** until required for the acquisition. Fund the new product lines by borrowing or raising additional equity finance.

Reason. The cash will be **needed at short notice** for the acquisition. It should be easy to raise finance for the new product lines from external sources.

....

Task 7.7

(a)

	Investment of £50,000	Interest 2% above base rate	Convertible within 60 days	Low/medium risk	No shares
Option 1	✓		✓	✓	✓
Option 2	✓	✓		✓	✓
Option 3		✓	✓	✓	✓

(b)

Option 1	
Option 2	
Option 3	
None of the options	✓

....

Chapter 8

Task 8.1

	Budget	Actual	Variance	Adv/Fav
	£	£	£	£
Receipts:				
Cash sales receipts	101,000	94,000	7,000	Adv
Credit sales receipts	487,000	475,000	12,000	Adv
Total receipts	588,000	569,000	19,000	Adv
Payments:				
Credit suppliers	303,000	294,000	9,000	Fav
Wages	155,000	162,000	7,000	Adv
Variable overheads	98,600	99,400	800	Adv
Fixed overheads	40,000	40,000	0	
Capital expenditure	0	45,000	45,000	Adv
Total payments	596,600	640,400	43,800	Adv
Net cash flow	(8,600)	(71,400)	62,800	Adv
Balance b/f	20,300	20,300	0	
Balance c/f	11,700	(51,100)	62,800	Adv

Task 8.2

(a)

	£
Budgeted closing bank balance	61,900
Surplus in cash sales	13,000
Shortfall in credit sales receipts	(25,000)
Increase in proceeds from sales from non-current (fixed) assets	22,000
Increase in payments to credit suppliers	(35,000)
No change in wages	0

	£
Increase in variable overheads	(7,400)
Increase in fixed overheads	(2,000)
Increase in purchase of non-current (fixed) assets	(46,000)
No change in dividend payments	0
Actual closing bank balance	(18,500)

(b) A

Although the other options may have resulted in a lower overdraft it is unlikely that any of these on their own are sufficient to reduce the deficit by £18,500.

Task 8.3

(a)

	Budget February	Actual February	Variance
	£	£	£
Cash receipts			
Receipts from sales	148,800	145,600	−3,200
Deposit account interest	100	100	-
Total cash receipts	**148,900**	**145,700**	**−3,200**
Cash payments			
Payments to suppliers	−41,600	−56,000	−14,400
Salaries	−43,000	−45,150	−2,150
Administration overheads	−30,000	−30,000	-
Capital expenditure	−20,000	−6,000	+14,000
Total payments	**−134,600**	**−137,150**	**−2,550**
Net cash flow	**14,300**	**8,550**	**−5,750**
Opening cash balance	−25,900	−25,900	-
Closing cash balance	**−11,600**	**−17,350**	**−5,750**

(b)

	£
Budgeted closing bank balance	−11,600
Surplus/<u>shortfall</u> in sales receipts	−3,200
Surplus/shortfall/<u>no change</u> in deposit account interest	0
<u>Increase</u>/decrease in payments to credit suppliers	−14,400
<u>Increase</u>/decrease in salaries	−2,150
Increase/decrease/<u>no change</u> in administration overheads	0
Increase/<u>decrease</u> in capital expenditure	+14,000
Actual closing bank balance	−17,350

(c)

Sales receipts	Loss of customers

Payments to suppliers	Increase in suppliers prices

Salaries	Bonus paid to staff

Capital expenditure	Negotiated credit with supplier of equipment, provided initial deposit paid in month of purchase

Task 8.4

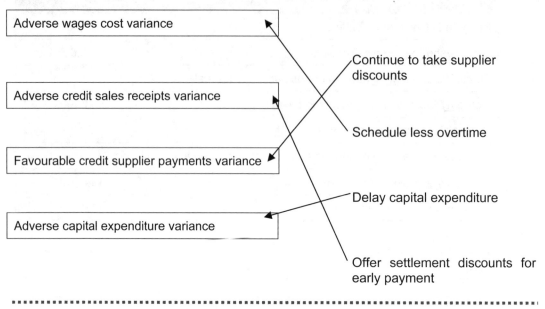

Adverse wages cost variance

Adverse credit sales receipts variance

Favourable credit supplier payments variance

Adverse capital expenditure variance

Continue to take supplier discounts

Schedule less overtime

Delay capital expenditure

Offer settlement discounts for early payment

SAMPLE ASSESSMENT
CASH MANAGEMENT

Time allowed: 2 hours

Sample Assessment

Task 1.1

(a) **Complete the diagram below of the working capital cycle by dragging and dropping the options into the correct box.**

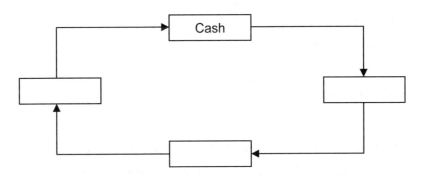

Options:

Payables (Creditors)
Receivables (Debtors)
Inventory (Stock)

(b) A business has an average inventory (stock) holding period of 94 days, receives payment from its customers in 58 days and pays its suppliers in 75 days.

What is the cash operating cycle in days for the business?

A 111 days
B 39 days
C 77 days
D 227 days

(c) **Selecting from the picklists, complete the following sentences:**

Over-trading can occur when a business has [too much/insufficient] working capital and over-capitalisation can occur when a business has [too much/insufficient] working capital.

Signs of over-trading include [slowly decreasing/rapidly decreasing/slowly increasing/rapidly increasing] sales volumes, [reducing/increasing] profit margins, [shorter/longer] debtor collection periods, [shorter/longer] creditor payment periods.

••

Task 1.2

(a) Cash receipts and payments take many different forms but they can be broadly categorised into regular, capital, exceptional and drawings.

Complete the table by dragging and dropping the correct description to match the type of cash receipt or cash payment.

Type of receipt or payment	Description
Capital payments	
Regular revenue receipts	
Drawings	
Exceptional payments	

Options:

Payments that relate to the proceeds from the disposal of non-current (fixed) assets

Payments that relate to the acquisition of non-current (fixed) assets

Payments made to the owners of the business

Payments received from the owners of the business

Income received from HM Revenue and Customs

Income received from the operating activities of the business that are expected to occur frequently

Income received from the operating activities of the business that are not expected to occur frequently

Payments arising from the operating activities of the business that are expected to occur frequently

Payments arising from the operating activities of the business that are not expected to occur frequently

Payments that do not arise from the operating activities of the business but that are expected to occur frequently

Payments that do not arise from the operating activities of the business and that are not expected to occur frequently

(b) J Wynn owns an office cleaning business and prepares quarterly income statements (profit and loss accounts) and statements of financial position (balance sheets). These are prepared on an accruals basis.

Cleaning materials are purchased when required and therefore very little inventory (stock) is maintained. All sales and purchases are made on credit terms.

The income statement for J Wynn's business for the quarter ended 31 December is as follows:

	£	£
Sales		182,400
Less: Purchases		(27,360)
Gross profit		155,040
Less: Expenses		
Wages	72,900	
Rent of office	12,650	
Office expenses	18,640	
Van expenses	24,118	
Van depreciation	4,190	
		(132,498)
		22,542

Extracts from the statements of financial position at 1 October and 31 December show the following:

Statement of financial position at	31 December £	1 October £
Receivables (Debtors)	16,400	21,620
Payables (Creditors)	1,124	760
Accruals – office expenses	241	119
Prepayments – van expenses	567	483
Prepayments – rent of office	1,450	1,200

Calculate the actual business cash receipts and cash payments for the quarter to 31 December.

	£
Sales receipts	
Purchases payments	
Wages paid	
Rent paid	
Office expenses	
Van expenses	
Van depreciation	

Task 1.3

A company is preparing its forecast sales and purchase information for the first quarter of next year.

The sales volume trend is to be identified using a 3-point moving average based on the actual monthly sales volumes for the current year.

(a) **Complete the table below to calculate the monthly sales volume trend and identify any monthly variations.**

	Sales volume (units)	Trend	Monthly variation (volume less trend)
August	9,360		
September	5,940		
October	5,220		
November	9,900		
December	6,480		

The monthly sales volume trend is [   ] units.

Additional information:

The selling price per unit has been set at £8.

Monthly purchases are estimated to be 40% of the value of the forecast sales.

(b) **Using the trend and the monthly variations identified in part (a) complete the table below to forecast the sales volume, sales value and purchase value for January of the next financial year.**

	Forecast trend	Variation	Forecast sales volume	Forecast sales £	Forecast purchases £
January					

Additional information

The company uses an industry wage rate index to forecast future monthly wage costs. Employees receive a pay increase in March each year. The current monthly wage cost of £6,220 was calculated when the wage index was 163. The forecast wage rate index for the next three months is:

January	179
February	186
March	193

(c) **If the company uses the forecast wage rate index what will the wage cost for March be, to the nearest £?**

A £7,365
B £5,253
C £6,454
D £5,994

Task 1.4

Sargent Enterprises has been trading for a number of years. The business has requested assistance with calculating sales receipts for entry into a cash budget.

Actual sales values are available for January and February and forecast figures have been produced for March to June.

Sargent Enterprises estimates that cash sales account for 12% of the total sales. The remaining 88% of sales are made on a credit basis.

(a) **Complete the table below to show the split of total sales between cash sales and credit sales.**

	Actual		Forecast			
	January	February	March	April	May	June
Total sales	37,500	42,000	45,000	51,000	58,000	63,750
Cash sales						
Credit sales						

Sargent Enterprises estimates that 60% of credit sales are received in the month after sale with the balance being received two months after sale. For example, 60% of January's credit sales are received in February with the balance being received in March.

(b) **Using the table below and your figures from part (a), calculate the timing of sales receipts ready to include in a cash budget for Sargent Enterprises.**

	Credit sales £	Cash received				
		February £	March £	April £	May £	June £
January						
February						
March						
April						
May						
Monthly credit sales receipts						

Task 1.5

Fortnum Ltd is preparing cash payment figures ready for inclusion in a cash budget. The following information is relevant to the payment patterns for purchases, wages and expenses.

- Purchases are calculated as 55% of the next month's forecast sales and are paid two months after the date of purchase. For example, purchases in July are based on the estimated sales for August and paid for in September.

	Actual			Forecast		
	July £	August £	September £	October £	November £	December £
Total sales	84,000	86,700	85,300	89,000	90,600	91,200

- Wages are paid in the month that they are incurred and expenses are paid in the month after they are incurred. The actual and forecast figures for wages and expenses are:

	Actual			Forecast		
	July £	August £	September £	October £	November £	December £
Wages	11,750	11,750	12,000	12,300	12,300	12,750
Expenses (excluding depreciation)	5,808	6,879	7,470	8,836	7,652	7,478

- A new machine is to be purchased in October at a total cost of £45,000. Payment for the machine is to be made in three equal monthly installments, beginning in October.

- The machine is to be depreciated monthly on a straight-line basis at 20% per annum.

Prepare an extract of the payments section of the cash budget for Fortnum Ltd for the three months ended December.

	October £	November £	December £
PAYMENTS			
Purchases			
Wages			
Expenses			
New machine			
Total payments			

Task 1.6

The cash budget for Goran Industries for the three months ended June has been partially completed. The following information is to be incorporated and the cash budget completed.

- A bank loan of £43,200 has been negotiated and this will be paid into the business bank account in April.

- The principle (capital) element of the bank loan (£43,200) is to be repaid in 48 equal monthly instalments beginning in May.

- The loan attracts 5% interest per annum calculated on the amount of the loan principle advanced in April. The annual interest charge is to be paid in equal monthly instalments beginning in May.

- When Goran Industries uses its bank overdraft facility interest is payable monthly and is estimated at 1% of the previous month's overdraft balance. The interest is to be rounded to the nearest £.

- At 1 April the balance of the bank account was £4,232.

Using the additional information above, complete the cash budget for Goran Industries for the three months ending June. Cash inflows should be entered as positive figures and cash outflows as negative figures. Zeroes must be entered where appropriate to achieve full marks.

	April £	May £	June £
RECEIPTS			
Cash sales	8,100	9,180	10,440
Credit sales	53,064	53,516	64,152
Bank loan		0	0
Total receipts			
PAYMENTS			
Purchases	−34,650	−37,125	−42,075
Wages	−18,000	−18,450	−18,450
Expenses	−10,318	−11,269	−13,254
Capital expenditure	0	−49,500	0
Bank loan capital repayment	0		
Bank loan interest	0		
Overdraft interest	0		

	April £	May £	June £
Total payments			
Net cash flow			
Opening bank balance			
Closing bank balance			

· ·

Task 2.1

A cash budget has been prepared for Inzyz Ltd for the next five periods.

The budget was prepared based on the following sales volumes and a selling price of £24 per item.

	Period 1	Period 2	Period 3	Period 4	Period 5
Sales volume (items)	1,150	1,200	1,230	1,260	1,300

The pattern of cash receipts used in the budget assumed 50% of sales were received in the month of sale and the remaining 50% in the month following sale.

In the light of current economic trends Inzyz Ltd needs to adjust its cash budget to take account of the following:

- The selling price from period 1 will be reduced by 15% per item.
- The pattern of sales receipts changes to 25% of sales received in the month of sale, 50% in the month following sale and the remaining 25% two months after sale.

(a) **Use the table below to calculate the effect of the changes in the forecast amounts and timing of cash receipts for periods 3, 4 and 5.**

	Period 1 (£)	Period 2 (£)	Period 3 (£)	Period 4 (£)	Period 5 (£)
Original value of forecast sales	27,600	28,800	29,520	30,240	31,200
Original timing of receipts			29,160	29,880	30,720
Revised value of forecast sales					
Revised timing of receipts					

Additional information

The company has managed to negotiate extended payment terms with its suppliers. The original budget was prepared on the basis of paying suppliers in the month following purchase. The revised payment terms allow for settlement of 30% in the month following purchase with the remaining payment two months after purchase.

The original budgeted purchase figures were:

	Period 1 (£)	Period 2 (£)	Period 3 (£)	Period 4 (£)	Period 5 (£)
Purchases	8,480	9,600	9,820	10,940	11,110

(b) **Use the table below to calculate the effect of the changes in the timing of purchase payments for periods 3, 4 and 5.**

	Period 3 (£)	Period 4 (£)	Period 5 (£)
Original timing of payments			
Revised timing of receipts			

Inzyz Ltd has always tried to operate without utilising a bank overdraft and the original cash budget identified that an overdraft would not be required for periods 3, 4 or 5.

(c) **Using your calculations from parts (a) and (b), complete the table to show the effect of the changes to sales receipts and purchase payments on the budgeted bank balance for periods 3, 4 and 5.**

	Period 3 (£)	Period 4 (£)	Period 5 (£)
Opening bank balance	3,790		
Changes in sales receipts			
Changes in purchase payments			
Closing bank balance			

···

Task 2.2

The quarterly budgeted and actual figures for an organisation are provided below:

	Budgeted £	Actual £
Receipts from receivables (debtors)	86,423	81,667
Cash sales	14,350	11,780
Payments to payables (creditors)	(42,618)	(44,791)
Cash purchases	(7,600)	(7,940)
Capital expenditure	–	(28,000)
Wages and salaries	(19,200)	(17,600)
General expenses	(24,650)	(22,464)
Net cash flow	6,705	(27,348)
Opening bank balance	4,200	4,200
Closing bank balance	10,905	(23,148)

(a) **Prepare a reconciliation of budgeted cash flow with actual cash flow for the quarter. Select the appropriate description for each entry.**

	£
Budgeted closing bank balance	
Surplus/Shortfall in receipts from receivables (debtors)	
Surplus/Shortfall in cash sales	
Increase/Decrease in payments to payables (creditors)	
Increase/Decrease in capital expenditure	
Increase/Decrease in cash payments	
Increase/Decrease in wages and salaries	
Increase/Decrease in general expenses	
Actual closing bank balance	

(b) **What actions could the organisation have taken to avoid an overdrawn bank balance?**

A   Chased customers to pay sooner and delayed payments to suppliers
B   Increased cash sales through better marketing
C   Delayed capital expenditure
D   Negotiated lower wages payments to employees

(c) Variances between budget and actual cash flows can occur for a number of reasons. There are also a variety of courses of action available to minimise adverse variances or benefit from favourable variances.

Match each cause of a variance listed on the left with a possible course of action from the list on the right.

Labour costs have increased	Improve credit control
Sales volumes have decreased	Change suppliers
Payments to suppliers are being made earlier	Reduce overtime working
Customers are taking more days to settle their debts	Negotiate early settlement discount
Prices of raw materials have increased	Improve the product

Task 2.3

(a) **Which of the following best describes the main features of an overdraft?**

    A   Interest rates are low; it is available for as long as required; it is useful for capital purchases.

    B   Interest rates are low; it is repayable on demand; it is useful for capital purchases.

    C   Interest rates are low; repayments can be negotiated; it is useful for capital purchases.

    D   Interest rates are high; repayments can be negotiated; it is a short-term form of finance.

    E   Interest rates are high; it is repayable on demand; it is a short-term form of finance.

    F   Interest rates are high; it is available for as long as required; it is a long-term form of finance.

(b) **Which of the following best describes the main features of a bank loan?**

    A   Interest rates are low; it is available for as long as required; it is useful for capital purchases.

    B   Interest rates are low; it is repayable on demand; it is useful for capital purchases.

    C   Interest rates are low; repayments can be negotiated; it is useful for capital purchases.

    D   Interest rates are high; repayments can be negotiated; it is a short-term form of finance.

    E   Interest rates are high; it is repayable on demand; it is a short-term form of finance.

    F   Interest rates are high; it is available for as long as required; it is a long-term form of finance.

(c) **Complete the sentences below using the picklists.**

A bank facility letter sets out the [draft/ possible/ legal/ illegal] rights and duties of [the bank/ the customer/ the bank and the customer] when the bank grants [an overdraft facility/ a bank loan/ overdrafts and loans].

The purpose of a facility letter is to protect the rights of [the bank/ the customer/ the bank and the customer].

Task 2.4

The three partner firm of Parry & Associates is planning to expand its production facilities. The expansion plans will require the purchase of new machinery at a cost of £78,000 and a working capital injection of £18,000.

The partnership has been seeking possible means of funding the expansion and has been offered three options:

Option 1   A bank loan of £78,000 secured on the new machinery. Capital repayments are to be made over four years in equal instalments. The interest rate is fixed at 6% per annum calculated on the capital balance outstanding at the beginning of each year.

An arrangement fee equal to 1% of the bank loan is payable at the beginning of the loan term.

The bank is also offering an overdraft facility of £19,500 which attracts an annual interest rate of 12%. The partners believe that they will require an average overdraft of £16,000 for eight months of the first year.

Option 2   A bank loan of £96,000 secured on the assets of the partnership. Principle (capital) repayments are to be made over four years, with a four month payment holiday at the beginning of the loan term. (This means that repayments of the principle will not begin until the fifth month after the loan is received by the partnership.)

The interest rate is fixed at 6½% per annum for the first two years and will then revert to a variable interest rate set at 3% above the base rate.

An arrangement fee equal to 0.75% of the bank loan is payable at the beginning of the loan term.

Under this option there will be no requirement for a bank overdraft facility.

Option 3   Each of the three partners will take out a personal secured loan of £32,000 repayable over five years at an interest rate of 2.5%. These monies will then be loaned to the partnership as increased capital. Interest of 4% per annum is payable by the partnership to the partners.

Under this option there will be no requirement for a bank overdraft facility.

An extract from the partnership policy in respect of raising finance states the following:

- The maximum overdraft facility that the partnership may obtain is £20,000.
- Interest payable by the partnership is to be kept as low as possible.
- Loan finance may be secured on the assets of the partnership.
- The partners should not give personal guarantees or security for loan finance.

(a) **Complete the table below to calculate the cost to the partnership for the first year of financing under each of the three options.**

	Loan Interest £	Arrangement fee £	Overdraft interest £	Total cost £
Option 1				
Option 2				
Option 3				

(b) **Which financing option should the partnership select taking account of the provision of the partnership policy?**

Option 1	
Option 2	
Option 3	
None of the options	

•••

Task 2.5

Use the picklists to complete the following sentences:

Certificates of deposit are certificates issued by [banks/ companies/ stock exchange/ local authority] that certify that an amount of money has been deposited and will be repaid at a specific date in the future. They [can/cannot] be traded on a market. They are considered to be a [low risk/high risk] investment.

Local authority short-term loans are certificates issued by [banks/ companies/ stock exchange/ local authorities] and backed by the government. They [can/cannot] be traded on a market. They are considered to be a [low risk/high risk] investment.

Government securities are also known as [gold-edged/ gilt-edged/ gilted] securities and [can/cannot] be traded. Interest rates are [fixed/variable] and these types of securities are considered to be [low risk/ high risk] because [they are/are not] backed by the government.

•••

Task 2.6

The investment manual of a treasury department in a large company has the following policy for investing surplus funds:

- The investment must be convertible to cash within 60 days.
- The maximum amount to be invested in any one type of investment is £50,000.
- The interest rate must be at least 2% above base rate which is currently 0.5%.
- The investment must not include shares.
- Only low or medium risk investments are to be selected.

Four possible investment options are available:

Option 1

Investment of £50,000 required; 90-day notice period; medium risk; investment portfolio includes shares; interest rate is 2.8% per annum.

Option 2

Maximum investment is £80,000 and minimum investment is £30,000; 30-day notice period; interest rate is 1.5% above base rate; low risk; does not include investment in shares.

Option 3

Investment portfolio comprises stocks and shares; high risk; projected interest rate is 7% and a minimum investment of £40,000 is required; 45-day notice period.

Option 4

Low risk; guaranteed return of 3% per annum; no stocks or shares; minimum investment of £52,000; 7-day notice period.

Complete the table below to show which of the policy requirements are met by each of the options. Use this table to recommend which of the options, if any, should be selected.

	Convertible within 60 days	Investment £50,000 or below	Interest rate 2% above base	Investment does not include shares	Risk
Option 1					
Option 2					
Option 3					
Option 4					

The company should select [Option 1/Option 2/Option 3/Option 4/ None of the options].

SAMPLE ASSESSMENT
CASH MANAGEMENT

ANSWERS

Sample Assessment Answers

Task 1.1

(a)

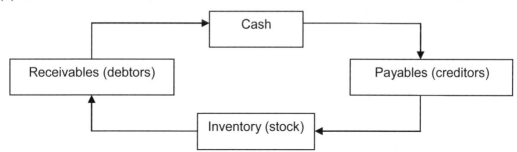

(b)   94 + 58 – 75 = 77 so correct choice is C

Note: incorrect answers calculated as:

94 – 58 + 75 = 111

58 + 75 – 94 = 39

94 + 58 + 75 = 227

(c)

Over-trading can occur when a business has <u>insufficient</u> working capital and over-capitalisation can occur when a business has <u>too much</u> working capital.

Signs of over-trading include <u>rapidly increasing</u> sales volumes, <u>reducing</u> profit margins, <u>longer</u> receivables' (debtor) collection periods, <u>longer</u> payables' (creditor) payment periods.

Task 1.2

(a)

Type of receipt or payment	Description
Capital payments	Payments that relate to the acquisition of non-current (fixed) assets
Regular revenue receipts	Income received from the operating activities of the business that are expected to occur frequently
Drawings	Payments made to the owners of the business
Exceptional payments	Payments that do not arise from the operating activities of the business and that are not expected to occur frequently

(b)

	£
Sales receipts	187,620
Purchases payments	26,996
Wages paid	72,900
Rent paid	12,900
Office expenses	18,518
Van expenses	24,202
Van depreciation	0

Workings

Sales receipts   = 182,400 + 21,620 – 16,400 = 187,620
Purchases payments = 27,360 + 760 – 1,124   = 26,996
Rent paid   = 12,650 – 1,200 + 1,450   = 12,900
Office expenses   = 18,640 + 119 – 241   = 18,518
Van expenses   = 24,118 – 483 + 567   = 24,202
Van depreciation   = 0 (this is not a cash expense)

Task 1.3

(a)

	Sales volume (units)	Trend	Monthly variation
August	9,360		
September	5,940	6,840	–900
October	5,220	7,020	–1,800
November	9,900	7,200	2,700
December	6,480		

The monthly sales volume trend is [180] units.

This is calculated as ((7,200 – 6,840)/2 interval gaps).

(b)

	Forecast trend	Variation	Forecast sales volume	Forecast sales £	Forecast purchases £
January	7,560	−1,800	5,760	46,080	18,432

(c) £6,220 ÷ 163 × 193 = 7,365 so the correct answer is A

Note: incorrect answers calculated as:

£6,220 ÷ 193 × 163 = 5,253

£6,220 ÷ 186 × 193 = 6,454

£6,220 ÷ 193 × 186 = 5,994

Task 1.4

(a)

	Actual		Forecast			
	January	February	March	April	May	June
Total sales	37,500	42,000	45,000	51,000	58,000	63,750
Cash sales (12%)	4,500	5,040	5,400	6,120	6,960	7,650
Credit sales (88%)	33,000	36,960	39,600	44,880	51,040	56,100

(b)

	Credit sales £	Cash received				
		February £	March £	April £	May £	June £
January	33,000	19,800	13,200			
February	36,960		22,176	14,784		
March	39,600			23,760	15,840	
April	44,880				26,928	17,952
May	51,040					30,624
	Monthly credit sales receipts		35,376	38,544	42,768	48,576

Task 1.5

	October £	November £	December £
PAYMENTS			
Purchases	46,915	48,950	49,830
Wages	12,300	12,300	12,750
Expenses	7,470	8,836	7,652
New machine	15,000	15,000	15,000
Total payments	81,685	85,086	85,232

Task 1.6

	April £	May £	June £
RECEIPTS			
Cash sales	8,100	9,180	10,440
Credit sales	53,064	53,516	64,152
Bank loan	43,200	0	0
Total receipts	104,364	62,696	74,592
PAYMENTS			
Purchases	−34,650	−37,125	−42,075
Wages	−18,000	−18,450	−18,450
Expenses	−10,318	−11,269	−13,254
Capital expenditure	0	−49,500	0
Bank loan capital repayment	0	−900	−900
Bank loan interest	0	−180	−180
Overdraft interest	0	0	−91
Total payments	−62,968	−117,424	−74,950
Net cash flow	41,396	−54,728	−358
Opening bank balance	4,232	45,628	−9,100
Closing bank balance	45,628	−9,100	−9,458

Task 2.1

(a)

	Period 1 (£)	Period 2 (£)	Period 3 (£)	Period 4 (£)	Period 5 (£)
Original value of forecast sales	27,600	28,800	29,520	30,240	31,200

			Period 3 (£)	Period 4 (£)	Period 5 (£)
Original timing of receipts			29,160	29,880	30,720
Revised value of forecast sales (£20.40 selling price per unit)	23,460	24,480	25,092	25,704	26,520

			Period 3 (£)	Period 4 (£)	Period 5 (£)
Revised timing of receipts (W1)			24,378	25,092	25,755
Increase/(decrease) in sales receipts (Note)			(4,782)	(4,788)	(4,965)

Workings
W1
Period 3 = (25% × 23,460) + (50% × 24,480) + (25% × 25,092) = 24,378
Period 4 = (25% × 24,480) + (50% × 25,092) + (25% × 25,704) = 25,092
Period 5 = (25% × 25,092) + (50% × 25,704) + (25% × 26,520) = 25,755

Note
This line of figures is not required to answer part (a) of the task but is here to show how the figures needed for part (c) of the task for changes in sales receipts are calculated.

(b)

	Period 3 (£)	Period 4 (£)	Period 5 (£)
Original timing of payments	9,600	9,820	10,940
Revised timing of receipts (W1)	8,816	9,666	10,156
Change in purchase payments (Note)	784	154	784

Workings

W1

Period 3 = (30% × 9,600) + (70% × 8,480) = 8,816
Period 4 = (30% × 9,820) + (70% × 9,600) = 9,666
Period 5 = (30% × 10,940) + (70% × 9,820) = 10,156

Note

This line of figures is not required to answer part (b) of the task but is here to show how the figures needed for part (c) of the task for changes in purchase payments are calculated.

(c)

	Period 3 (£)	Period 4 (£)	Period 5 (£)
Opening bank balance	3,790	(208)	(4,842)
Changes in sales receipts (from part (a))	(4,782)	(4,788)	(4,965)
Changes in purchase payments (from part (b))	784	154	784
Closing bank balance	(208)	(4,842)	(9,023)

....

Task 2.2

(a)

	£
Budgeted closing bank balance	10,905
Shortfall in receipts from receivables (debtors)	(4,756)
Shortfall in cash sales	(2,570)
Increase in payments to payables (creditors)	(2,173)
Increase in capital expenditure	(28,000)
Increase in cash payments	(340)
Decrease in wages and salaries	1,600
Decrease in general expenses	2,186
Actual closing bank balance	(23,148)

(b) C

Note: Although the other options could have resulted in a lower overdraft they are not sufficient in and of themselves to reduce the deficit by £23,148.

(c)

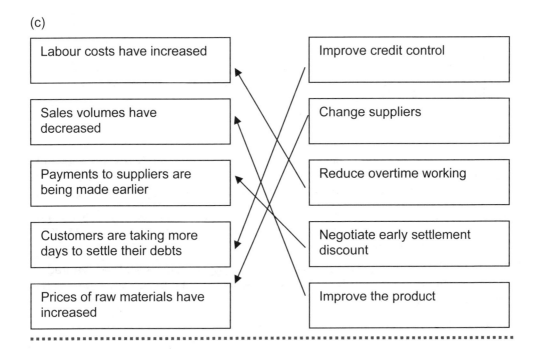

Labour costs have increased	Improve credit control
Sales volumes have decreased	Change suppliers
Payments to suppliers are being made earlier	Reduce overtime working
Customers are taking more days to settle their debts	Negotiate early settlement discount
Prices of raw materials have increased	Improve the product

Task 2.3

(a) E

(b) C

(c) A bank facility letter sets out the <u>legal</u> rights and duties of <u>the bank and the customer</u> when the bank grants <u>overdrafts and loans</u>.

The purpose of a facility letter is to protect the rights <u>the bank and the customer</u>.

Task 2.4

(a)

	Loan interest £	Arrangement fee £	Overdraft interest £	Total cost £
Option 1	4,680	780	1,280	6,740
Option 2	6,240	720	0	6,960
Option 3	3,840	0	0	3,840

(b)

Option 1	✓
Option 2	
Option 3	
None of the options	

..

Task 2.5

Certificates of deposit are certificates issued by <u>banks</u> that certify that an amount of money has been deposited and will be repaid at a specific date in the future. They <u>can</u> be traded on a market. They are considered to be a <u>low risk</u> investment.

Local authority short-term loans are certificates issued by <u>local authorities</u> and backed by the government. They <u>can</u> be traded on a market. They are considered to be a <u>low risk</u> investment.

Government securities are also known as <u>gilt-edged</u> securities and <u>can</u> be traded. Interest rates are <u>fixed</u> and these types of securities are considered to be <u>low risk</u> because <u>they are</u> backed by the government.

..

Task 2.6

	Convertible within 60 days	Investment £50,000 or below	Interest rate 2% above base	Investment does not include shares	Risk
Option 1		✓	✓		✓
Option 2	✓	✓		✓	✓
Option 3	✓	✓	✓		
Option 4	✓		✓	✓	✓

The company should select <u>none of the options</u>.

..

PRACTICE ASSESSMENT 1
CASH MANAGEMENT

Time allowed: 2 hours

Cash Management Practice Assessment 1

Task 1.1

FH Ltd is preparing its cash budget for the three months ending September 20X6. The following information about the sales of its product in that period is given.

(1) Sales are expected to be 6,800 units in July, 7,000 units in August and 7,300 units in September.

(2) The current price of a unit is £13.20 but there is to be a 5% price increase from 1 August 20X6.

(3) Although the policy is for all trade customers to pay within 30 days, for budgetary purposes it is assumed that 20% of customers pay one month after the date of sale, 70% pay two months after the date of sale and 10% pay three months after the date of sale.

(4) Assume that receivables (debtors) at 30 June of £166,710 will pay as follows:

In July	£87,248
In August	£70,618
In September	£8,844
	£166,710

Complete the table below to calculate the receipts from credit customers for the three months ending in September.

	Workings	July £	August £	September £
Total receipts from customers				

Task 1.2

PL Ltd is a company which manufactures fence panels. Production is budgeted to be 7,100 units in July, 7,300 units in August and 7,600 units in September.
You are given the following information regarding the purchases for the company:

(1) The cost of a strip of wood is expected to remain at £0.20 per strip for the next six months.

(2) Each fence panel requires 25 strips of wood.

(3) Wood inventory (stock) at 30 June 20X6 are 160,000 strips valued at £32,000.

(4) The plan is to reduce inventory (stock) of wood to 150,000 strips at the end of August and 120,000 strips at the end of September.

(a) **Complete the table below to calculate the purchases budget in units and in £ for the three-month period ending in September.**

	Workings	July	August	September
		Strips of wood	Strips of wood	Strips of wood
Production requirements				
Opening inventory (stock)				
Closing inventory (stock)				
Purchases in units				
		£	£	£
Purchases in £				

All purchases of wood will continue to be paid for one month in arrears as at present. The payables (creditors) amount at 30 June 20X6 for purchases of wood made during June was £33,500.

(b) **Complete the table below to calculate the payments made to suppliers in each of the three months ending in September.**

	Workings	July	August	September
		£	£	£

Each panel takes 20 minutes of labour time to manufacture and the production staff are currently paid £7.50 per hour. It is expected that this will increase to £7.80 per hour from 1 September 20X6.

(c) **Complete the table below to calculate the wages cost for each of the three months ending in September.**

	Workings	July	August	September
		£	£	£

Task 1.3

The cash budget for GI Ltd for the three months ended September has been partially completed. The following information is to be incorporated and the cash budget completed.

Additional information

- Fixed production overheads are expected to remain at £14,000 for July 20X6 which includes £4,000 of depreciation. The overheads other than depreciation are expected to increase by 5% from 1 August 20X6.

- Repairs and maintenance costs should be budgeted at an average of £2,500 per month.

- Sales department costs are expected to be £4,000 per month including depreciation of £800 per month.

- Capital expenditure of £20,000 should be budgeted for in August 20X6.

- The cash balance at 30 June 20X6 was £23,900.

Using the additional information above, complete the cash budget for GI Ltd for the three months ending in September. Cash inflows should be entered as positive figures and cash outflows as negative figures. Zeroes must be entered where appropriate to achieve full marks.

Cash budget for three months ending 30 September 20X6

	July £	August £	September £
Receipts:			
Receipts from customers	**104,697**	**106,284**	**109,296**
Payments:			
Payments to suppliers	−50,200	−52,600	−51,400
Wages	−21,300	−21,900	−23,700
Production overheads			
Selling overheads			
Repairs and maintenance			
Capital expenditure			
Total payments:			
Net cash flow			
Opening cash balance			
Closing cash balance			

Task 1.4

Complete the table by ticking the correct boxes to show whether an item affects cash or profit.

	Cash	Profit
Sales on credit		
Purchase of non-current (fixed) asset		
Depreciation		
Accrual of expenses		
Receipts from credit customers		
Dividend		

Task 1.5

A business had sales for the period of £68,700, purchases of £33,500 and expenses of £12,400.

The following figures have been taken from the Statement of Financial Position (balance sheet):

	Closing figures	Opening figures
Receivables (debtors)	£6,200	£4,300
Payables (creditors)	£1,100	£2,100
Prepaid expenses	£1,900	£1,200

Calculate the actual cash receipts and payments for the period.

	£
Sales receipts	
Purchases payments	
Expense payments	

Task 1.6

A company uses an industry wage rate index to forecast future monthly wage costs. The current monthly wage cost of £10,660 was calculated when the wage index was 110. The forecast wage index for June is 144.

If the company uses the forecast wage rate index, what will the wage cost for June be to the nearest £?

A   £15,350
B   £8,143
C   £13,955
D   £11,726

Task 2.1

A cash budget has been prepared for KL Ltd for the next five periods.

The budget was prepared based on the following sales volumes and a selling price of £10 per item.

	Period 1	Period 2	Period 3	Period 4	Period 5
Sales volume (items)	1,400	1,500	1,450	1,390	1,300

The pattern of cash receipts used in the budget assumed 60% of sales were paid for by customers in the month following the sale and the remaining 40% of customers paid two months after the sale.

The company is considering introducing a settlement discount of 2% for payments made in the month of the sale. This policy is expected to result in 50% of customers paying in the month of the sale, 10% paying in the month following the sale and the remaining 40% paying two months following the sale.

(a) **Complete the table below to calculate the forecast receipts from customers for each of periods 3, 4 and 5 under the current payment system from customers.**

	Workings	Period 3 £	Period 4 £	Period 5 £
Total receipts from customers				

(b) **Complete the table below to calculate the forecast receipts from customers for each of periods 3, 4 and 5 if the system of settlement discounts is introduced.**

	Workings	Period 3 £	Period 4 £	Period 5 £

	Workings	Period 3 £	Period 4 £	Period 5 £
Total receipts from customers				

(c) **Complete the table below to show the effects of introducing the discount system.**

	Period 3 £	Period 4 £	Period 5 £
Original receipts from customers			
Revised receipts from customers			
Increase/(decrease) in sales receipts			

Task 2.2

Given below is the cash budget for the three months ended 30 June 20X6 for an organisation. You are also given the actual cash flows for the three-month period.

Cash budget for the three months ended 30 June 20X6

	April £	May £	June £
Receipts from customers	91,500	96,700	92,400
Payments to suppliers	(31,400)	(28,800)	(30,100)
Wages	(16,250)	(16,500)	(16,750)
Production overheads	(10,000)	(10,000)	(10,000)
Selling overheads	(3,300)	(3,000)	(3,000)
Repairs and maintenance	(1,100)	(1,500)	(1,100)
Capital expenditure	0	0	0
Dividend	–	–	(30,000)
Cash flow for the month	29,450	36,900	1,450
Opening cash balance	41,100	70,550	107,450
Closing cash balance	70,550	107,450	108,900

Actual cash flows

The actual cash flows for each of the three months ended 30 June 20X6 were as follows:

	April	May	June
	£	£	£
Receipts from customers	86,500	91,200	84,400
Payments to suppliers	(33,200)	(33,200)	(32,700)
Wages	(16,250)	(16,500)	(16,750)
Production overheads	(10,000)	(10,000)	(10,000)
Selling overheads	(3,100)	(3,400)	(3,500)
Repairs and maintenance	(4,100)	(3,900)	(2,700)
Capital expenditure		(50,000)	
Dividend	–	–	(30,000)
Cash flow for the month	19,850	(25,800)	(11,250)
Opening cash balance	41,100	60,950	35,150
Closing cash balance	60,950	35,150	23,900

Prepare a reconciliation of the budgeted cash balance with the actual cash balance at 30 June 20X6. Select the appropriate description for each entry by highlighting it.

	£
Budgeted closing cash balance	
Surplus/shortfall in receipts from customers	
Increase/decrease in payments to suppliers	
Increase/decrease in selling overheads	
Increase/decrease in repairs and maintenance	
Increase/decrease in capital expenditure	
Actual closing cash balance	

Task 2.3

For each of the following significant deviations from a cash budget given on the left match a possible course of action that could have been taken to avoid each of these variances from the list on the right.

Deviation in receipts from customers

Delay expenditure or find an alternative method of funding

Deviation in payments to suppliers

Improve credit control procedures

Change in repairs and maintenance payments

Arrange a fixed price maintenance contract

Change in capital expenditure

Negotiate credit terms for payment

Task 2.4

In the past a company has invested surplus funds in a variety of Treasury stocks and also in fixed term deposits with the bank.

(a) **Selecting from the picklists, complete the following sentences.**

Gilt-edged securities or gilts are [marketable/non-marketable] British Government securities. They pay a [variable/fixed/capped] amount of interest and are available with varying maturity dates which is the date [on which they will be redeemed/they must be kept until].

(b) **If interest rates increase what affect will this have on the interest rate for gilt-edged stocks and a bank deposit account?**

	Gilt-edged stocks	Bank deposit account
A	Increase	No change
B	Decrease	No change
C	No change	Increase
D	No change	Decrease

(c) **If interest rates increase what affect will this have on the redemption value for gilt-edged stocks and a bank deposit account?**

	Gilt-edged stocks	Bank deposit account
A	Increase	No change
B	Decrease	No change
C	No change	Increase
D	No change	Decrease

Task 2.5

(a) **Complete the table by entering each of the advantages against the correct type of financing.**

Type of finance	Advantages
Bank loan	
Overdraft	

Security not normally required

Useful to fund working capital

Precise amount required does not need to be known

Covenants not normally included

Relatively low cost

Repayments can be negotiated

(b) **The directors of FH Panels Ltd have identified the opportunity to purchase a freehold property at a cost of £1,100,000. They will also require additional working capital for the project of £100,000.**

What would normally be the best method of financing these two elements of the project?

	Freehold property	Working capital
A	Overdraft	Overdraft
B	Bank loan	Bank loan
C	Bank loan	Overdraft
D	Overdraft	Bank loan

Task 2.6

Complete the table to below to indicate the effect that certain actions by a company would have on any overdraft finance.

	Increase overdraft (tick)	Decrease overdraft (tick)
Increase inventory (stock) levels		
Improve credit control procedures		
Increase quantity of sales		
Drawings taken by the owner		

PRACTICE ASSESSMENT 1
CASH MANAGEMENT

ANSWERS

Cash Management Practice Assessment 1 – Answers

Task 1.1

Receipts from credit customers

	Workings	July £	August £	September £
Receivables (debtors) at 30 June		87,248	70,618	8,844
July sales	6,800 × 13.20 × 20%		17,952	
	6,800 × 13.20 × 70%			62,832
August sales	7,000 × 13.20 × 1.05 × 20%			19,404
Total receipts from customers		**87,248**	**88,570**	**91,080**

Task 1.2

(a) Purchases budget

	Workings	July Strips of wood	August Strips of wood	September Strips of wood
Production requirements	7,100 × 25	177,500		
	7,300 × 25		182,500	
	7,600 × 25			190,000
Opening inventory (stock)		(160,000)	(160,000)	(150,000)
Closing inventory (stock)		160,000	150,000	120,000
Purchases in units		**177,500**	**172,500**	**160,000**
		£	£	£
Purchases in £ (units × £0.20)		**35,500**	**34,500**	**32,000**

(b)   **Payments to suppliers**

	Workings	July	August	September
		£	£	£
Opening payable (creditor)		33,500		
July purchases			35,500	
August purchases				34,500

(c)   **Wages payments**

	Workings	July	August	September
		£	£	£
July	7,100/3 × £7.50	17,750		
August	7,300/3 × £7.50		18,250	
September	7,600/3 × £7.80			19,760

Task 1.3

Cash budget for three months ending 30 September 20X6

	July £	August £	September £
Receipts:			
Receipts from customers	**104,697**	**106,284**	**109,296**
Payments:			
Payments to suppliers	−50,200	−52,600	−51,400
Wages	−21,300	−21,900	−23,700
Production overheads	−10,000	−10,500	−10,500
Selling overheads	−3,200	−3,200	−3,200
Repairs and maintenance	−2,500	−2,500	−2,500
Capital expenditure	0	−20,000	0
Total payments:	**−87,200**	**−110,700**	**−91,300**
Net cash flow	17,497	−4,416	17,996
Opening cash balance	23,900	41,397	36,981
Closing cash balance	41,397	36,981	54,977

Task 1.4

	Cash	Profit
Sales on credit		✓
Purchase of non-current (fixed) asset	✓	
Depreciation		✓
Accrual of expenses		✓
Receipts from credit customers	✓	
Dividend	✓	

Task 1.5

	£
Sales receipts (68,700 + 4,300 – 6,200)	66,800
Purchases payments (33,500 + 2,100 – 1,100)	34,500
Expense payments (12,400 – 1,200 + 1,900)	13,100

Task 1.6

C   £10,660 x 144/110   =   £13,955

Task 2.1

(a)

	Period 3 £	Period 4 £	Period 5 £
Period 1 sales 1,400 × £10 × 40%	5,600		
Period 2 sales 1,500 × £10 × 60%	9,000		
Period 2 sales 1,500 × £10 × 40%		6,000	
Period 3 sales 1,450 × £10 × 60%		8,700	
Period 3 sales 1,450 × £10 × 40%			5,800
Period 4 sales 1,390 × £10 × 60%			8,340
Total receipts from customers	**14,600**	**14,700**	**14,140**

(b)

	Period 3 £	Period 4 £	Period 5 £
Period 1 sales 1,400 × £10 × 40%	5,600		
Period 2 sales 1,500 × £10 × 10%	1,500		
Period 3 sales 1,450 × £10 × 50% × 98%	7,105		
Period 2 sales 1,500 × £10 × 40%		6,000	
Period 3 sales 1,450 × £10 × 10%		1,450	
Period 4 sales 1,390 × £10 × 50% × 98%		6,811	
Period 3 sales 1,450 × £10 × 40%			5,800
Period 4 sales 1,390 × £10 × 10%			1,390
Period 5 sales 1,300 × £10 × 50% × 98%			6,370
Total receipts from customers	**14,205**	**14,261**	**13,560**

(c)

	Period 3 £	Period 4 £	Period 5 £
Original receipts from customers	14,600	14,700	14,140
Revised receipts from customers	14,205	14,261	13,560
Increase/(decrease) in sales receipts	(395)	(439)	(580)

Task 2.2

	£
Budgeted closing cash balance	108,900
Shortfall in receipts from customers	(18,500)
Increase in payments to suppliers	(8,800)
Increase in selling overheads	(700)
Increase in repairs and maintenance	(7,000)
Increase in capital expenditure	(50,000)
Actual closing cash balance	23,900

Task 2.3

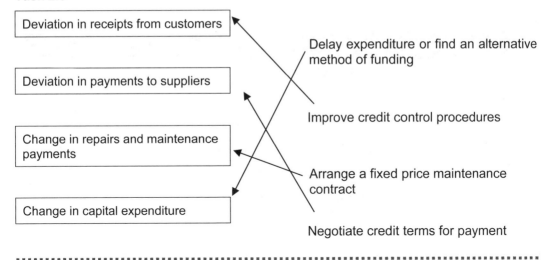

Deviation in receipts from customers	Delay expenditure or find an alternative method of funding
Deviation in payments to suppliers	Improve credit control procedures
Change in repairs and maintenance payments	Arrange a fixed price maintenance contract
Change in capital expenditure	Negotiate credit terms for payment

Task 2.4

(a) Gilt-edged securities or gilts are <u>marketable</u> British Government securities. They pay a <u>fixed</u> amount of interest and are available with varying maturity dates which is the date <u>on which they will be redeemed</u>.

(b) C

Both a bank deposit account and gilts carry a stated rate of interest. However, they will be affected differently by changes in base interest rates.

With the bank deposit account if base rates change then the interest payable on the deposit will also normally change. However, the interest rate on the gilts will remain the same.

(c) B

If interest rates increase the amount deposited in the bank account will not be affected and when the deposit matures the initial deposit will be the amount returned plus any accumulated interest.

However, gilts are marketable securities and as such their market value will fluctuate with changes in base rates. If the base rate of interest increases then the market value of any amount invested in gilts will fall. Whereas if market interest rates decrease the value of gilts will increase.

Task 2.5

(a)

Type of finance	Advantages
Bank loan	Relatively low cost
	Repayments can be negotiated
Overdraft	Security not normally required
	Useful to fund working capital
	Precise amount required does not need to be known
	Covenants not normally included

(b)   C

Task 2.6

	Increase overdraft (tick)	Decrease overdraft (tick)
Increase inventory (stock) levels	✓	
Improve credit control procedures		✓
Increase quantity of sales		✓
Drawings taken by the owner	✓	

PRACTICE ASSESSMENT 2
CASH MANAGEMENT

Time allowed: 2 hours

Cash Management Practice Assessment 2

Task 1.1

Happy Chefs Ltd, a catering company providing catering and meals for corporate and private clients, is preparing its cash budget for the first three months of 20X6.

January credit sales will be £104,000, February should be £140,000 and March £155,000. Cash inflows from sales invoices will be as follows:

- 40% in the month the invoice is issued
- 50% in the month after the invoice is issued
- 10% two months after the invoice is issued

Receivables (debtors) at 31 December 20X5 were £160,000 and of these it is anticipated that £125,000 will be received in January and the remainder in February.

From 1 February the company is opening a factory sales outlet for sales to the public of pre-packaged foods. In the early months sales for cash are expected to total £800 a month.

Complete the table below to calculate the receipts from sales for the three months ending in March.

	Workings	January £	February £	March £
Cash sales				
Opening receivables (debtors)				
January sales				
February sales				
March sales				
Total receipts from sales				

Task 1.2

A company is preparing its cash budget for the first three months of 20X6. The following information is known regarding forecast cash payments. The receipts have already been calculated and are given in the cash budget below.

- Purchases were £70,000 in December and are expected to be £41,600 in January, £56,000 in February and £62,000 in March. These purchases are paid for in the month after purchase.

- Salaries are currently £43,000 but are due to rise by 5% from 1 March.

- Administration costs will be £27,000 in January but due to a rent increase will go up by £3,000 from 1 February onwards.

- The company is investing in new equipment and there is to be a down payment of £20,000 on 1 February and a monthly payment thereafter of £6,000.

- The cash balance at 31 December 20X5 was an overdraft of £39,400 (ignore any interest on the overdraft.)

Prepare a monthly cash budget for the company for the three months to March.

	January £	February £	March £
Cash receipts			
Receipts from sales	153,400	148,800	145,600
Deposit account interest	100	100	100
Total cash receipts	**153,500**	**148,900**	**145,700**
Cash payments			
Payments to suppliers			
Salaries			
Administration overheads			
Capital expenditure			
Total payments			
Net cash flow			
Opening cash balance			
Closing cash balance			

Task 1.3

A company is trying to estimate its production volumes for one of its products for the first three months of 20X6. This to be done by calculating a trend using the actual monthly production volumes for 20X5 and a 3-point moving average.

(a) **Complete the table below to calculate the monthly production volume trend and identify any monthly variations.**

	Production volume	Trend	Monthly variation (volume less trend)
	Units	Units	Units
January	90,000		
February	98,000	100,000	−2,000
March	112,000	102,000	10,000
April	96,000	104,000	−8,000
May	104,000	106,000	−2,000
June	118,000	108,000	10,000
July	102,000	110,000	−8,000
August	110,000	112,000	−2,000
September	124,000	114,000	10,000
October	108,000	116,000	−8,000
November	116,000	118,000	−2,000
December	130,000		

The monthly sales volume trend is [2,000] units.

(b) **Using the trend and the monthly variations identified in part (a) complete the table below for forecast sales volume for January, February and March of the next financial year.**

	Forecast trend	Variation	Forecast sales volume
	Units	Units	Units
January	122,000	−8,000	114,000
February	124,000	−2,000	122,000
March	126,000	10,000	136,000

Task 1.4

The accountant of a company has prepared a budgeted Income Statement (profit and loss account) for the month of April 20X6 and a Statement of Financial Position (balance sheet) as at 30 April 20X6.

Extracts from the Income Statement are as follows:

	£
Sales	170,000
Purchases	72,000
Factory rent	31,000
Administrative expenses	14,000
Delivery lorry expenses	16,000
Delivery lorry depreciation	3,000

Extracts from the Statement of Financial Position at 1 April and 30 April are as follows:

	30 April	1 April
Receivables (debtors)	39,000	32,000
Payables (creditors)	15,000	17,000
Prepaid factory rent	7,000	6,000
Accrued administrative expenses	2,000	1,000
Accrued delivery lorry expenses	4,000	2,000

Calculate the actual cash receipts and payments for the month of April.

	£
Receipts for sales	
Payments for purchases	
Factory rent paid	
Administrative expenses paid	
Delivery lorry expenses paid	
Depreciation	

Task 1.5

Which of the following describes the cash operating cycle?

A   Inventory (stock) – receivables (debtors) + cash
B   Receivables (debtors) – payables (creditors) + inventory (stock) + cash
C   Cash + inventory (stock) – payables (creditors)
D   Receivables (debtors) + inventory (stock) + cash + payables (creditors)

Task 1.6

Selecting from the picklists complete the following sentences.

Over-trading occurs when a business has [too much/too little] working capital.

Over-capitalisation occurs when a business has [too much/too little] working capital.

Task 2.1

Given below are the budgeted and actual cash flows for a catering company for the month of December 20X5.

Complete the table below to calculate each variance between actual and budget and state whether it is favourable or adverse.

	Actual	Budget	Variance	Fav/Adv
	£	£	£	£
Sales receipts	154,000	175,000		
Food costs	–72,500	–64,000		
Salaries	–43,000	–43,000		
Administrative costs	–25,400	–27,600		
Capital expenditure	–64,000	–18,000		
Dividend	–20,000	0		
Deposit account interest	100	100		
Net cash flow	–70,800	22,500		
Opening cash balance	31,400	30,000		
Closing cash balance	–39,400	52,500		

Task 2.2

For each variance listed below on the left, match it to a possible cause from the list on the right.

| Sales receipts |

| Materials costs |

| Administrative costs |

| Capital expenditure |

| Dividend |

Unplanned expenditure

Loss of customers

Unplanned discretionary payment

Increase in suppliers prices

Cost cutting

....

Task 2.3

Complete the table by entering the actions which could have reduced the overdraft.

Action to reduce overdraft	

Delayed payment to suppliers
Delayed capital expenditure
Increased credit period to customers
Increased levels of inventory (stock)
Delayed dividend
Took out a bank loan for capital expenditure

....

Task 2.4

Using the picklists, complete the following sentences.

Primary banks are those which [do/do not] take part in the banking clearing system.

When a customer of a bank has an overdraft then the bank is the [receivable (debtor)/payable (creditor)] in the relationship.

A bank overdraft is [for a set period of time/repayable on demand].

A primary market is one where [new financial instruments are issued/ trading in existing financial instruments takes place].

One method of repaying a loan is by [bubble repayments/balloon repayments/gun repayments].

A floating charge is on the [non-current (fixed) assets/ current assets] of the business.

A covenant in a loan agreement is [the terms of repayment/the way in which interest will be charged/obligations on the receiver of the loan].

When investing funds as a general rule risk and return are related: the higher the risk of an investment, the [higher/lower] will be its anticipated return.

···

Task 2.5

Complete the table by entering the correct description to match the investment described.

Certificates of deposit	
Commercial paper	
Gilts	
Local authority stocks	
Bill of exchange	

Unconditional order in writing from one person to another

Marketable British Government securities

IOUs issued by large companies which can be either held to maturity or sold to third parties before maturity

Marketable securities with a slightly higher yield than government stocks

£50,000 or more for a fixed term which can be sold earlier than maturity

···

Task 2.6

The directors of a company are considering an expansion project which will require £500,000 of capital expenditure and £80,000 of additional working capital. The finance director has been investigating methods of raising this finance and has found three potential options.

Option 1   A bank loan for £580,000 secured on the non-current (fixed) assets of the company. The loan is to be repaid in equal instalments over a five-year period and has a fixed rate of interest for the first year of 4.8%. Thereafter the rate of interest will be variable at 2.2% above the base rate. There will be an arrangement fee for the loan of 0.7% at the start of the loan term.

Option 2   The five directors will each take out a personal secured loan of £100,000 at an annual interest rate of 5%. This money will then be loaned to the company and the personal interest cost for the directors recouped from the company. The company will require an overdraft facility of £80,000 which has been authorised by the bank at an annual rate of 10%. It is believed that in the first year only £50,000 on average will be required of this overdraft facility and only for the last seven months of the year.

Option 3   A bank loan for £500,000 could be taken out secured on the value of the current assets of the business. The loan will be repaid in equal instalments over five years and the interest is at a fixed rate of 6% based upon the outstanding capital balance at the start of the year. An arrangement fee of 0.5% of the bank loan is payable at the beginning of the loan term. The overdraft will also be required under this option and the details will be same as for option 2.

The Articles of Association of the company include the following in respect of the raising of finance:

- The company must not accept loans from officers or directors of the company.

- Any security given for loans must be floating charges.

- The maximum overdraft allowed is £100,000.

- The interest cost to the company of any financing options should be kept as low as possible.

(a) **Complete the table below to calculate the cost to the company for the first year of financing under each of the three options.**

	Arrangement fee £	Loan interest £	Overdraft interest £	Total cost £
Option 1				
Option 2				
Option 3				

(b) **Which financial option should the company select taking account of the provisions of the Articles of Association ?**

Option 1	
Option 2	
Option 3	
None of the options	

PRACTICE ASSESSMENT 2
CASH MANAGEMENT

ANSWERS

Cash Management Practice Assessment 2 – Answers

Task 1.1

Receipts from sales

	Workings	January	February	March
		£	£	£
Cash sales		800	800	800
Opening receivables (debtors)		125,000	35,000	
January sales	104,000 × 40%	41,600		
	104,000 × 50%		52,000	
	104,000 × 10%			10,400
February sales	140,000 × 40%		56,000	
	140,000 × 50%			70,000
March sales	155,000 × 40%			62,000
Total receipts from sales		**167,400**	**143,800**	**143,200**

Task 1.2

Cash budget for three months ending 31 March 20X6

	January	February	March
	£	£	£
Cash receipts			
Receipts from sales	153,400	148,800	145,600
Deposit account interest	100	100	100
Total cash receipts	**153,500**	**148,900**	**145,700**
Cash payments			
Payments to suppliers	–70,000	–41,600	–56,000
Salaries	–43,000	–43,000	–45,150
Administration overheads	–27,000	–30,000	–30,000

	January	February	March
	£	£	£
Capital expenditure		−20,000	−6,000
Total payments	**−140,000**	**−134,600**	**−137,150**
Net cash flow	**13,500**	**14,300**	**8,550**
Opening cash balance	−39,400	−25,900	−11,600
Closing cash balance	**−25,900**	**−11,600**	**−3,050**

Task 1.3

(a)

	Production volume	Trend	Monthly variation (volume less trend)
	Units	Units	Units
January	90,000		
February	98,000	100,000	−2,000
March	112,000	102,000	+10,000
April	96,000	104,000	−8,000
May	104,000	106,000	−2,000
June	118,000	108,000	+10,000
July	102,000	110,000	−8,000
August	110,000	112,000	−2,000
September	124,000	114,000	+10,000
October	108,000	116,000	−8,000
November	116,000	118,000	−2,000
December	130,000		

The monthly sales volume trend is $\boxed{2,000}$ units.

This is calculated as ((£118,000 − £100,000)/9 interval gaps).

(b)

	Forecast trend	Variation	Forecast sales volume
	Units	Units	Units
January (118,000 + (2 × 2000))	122,000	−8,000	114,000
February (118,000 + (3 × 2,000)	124,000	−2,000	122,000
March (118,000 + (4 × 3,000))	126,000	+10,000	136,000

Task 1.4

	£
Receipts for sales	163,000
Payments for purchases	74,000
Factory rent paid	32,000
Administrative expenses paid	13,000
Delivery lorry expenses paid	14,000
Depreciation	0

Workings

Receipts for sales	=	170,000 + 32,000 − 39,000	=	163,000
Payments for purchases	=	72,000 + 17,000 − 15,000	=	74,000
Factory rent paid	=	31,000 − 6,000 + 7,000	=	32,000
Administrative expenses	=	14,000 + 1,000 − 2,000	=	13,000
Lorry expenses	=	16,000 + 2,000 − 4,000	=	14,000
Depreciation	=	0 (this is not a cash expense)		

Task 1.5

B

Task 1.6

Over-trading occurs when a business has <u>too little</u> working capital.

Over-capitalisation occurs when a business has <u>too much</u> working capital.

Task 2.1

	Actual	Budget	Variance	Fav/Adv
	£	£	£	£
Sales receipts	154,000	175,000	21,000	Adv
Food costs	−72,500	−64,000	8,500	Adv
Salaries	−43,000	−43,000	0	
Administrative costs	−25,400	−27,600	2,200	Fav
Capital expenditure	−64,000	−18,000	46,000	Adv
Dividend	−20,000	0	20,000	Adv
Deposit account interest	100	100	0	
Net cash flow	−70,800	22,500	93,300	Adv
Opening cash balance	31,400	30,000	1,400	Fav
Closing cash balance	−39,400	52,500	91,900	Adv

Task 2.2

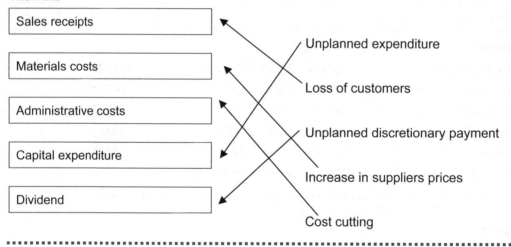

Sales receipts

Materials costs

Administrative costs

Capital expenditure

Dividend

Unplanned expenditure

Loss of customers

Unplanned discretionary payment

Increase in suppliers prices

Cost cutting

Task 2.3

Actions to reduce overdraft	Delayed payments to suppliers
	Delayed capital expenditure
	Delayed dividend
	Took out a bank loan for capital expenditure

Task 2.4

Primary banks are those which <u>do</u> take part in the banking clearing system.

When a customer of a bank has an overdraft then the bank is the receivable (<u>debtor</u>) in the relationship.

A bank overdraft <u>is repayable on demand</u>.

A primary market is one where <u>new financial instruments are issued</u>.

One method of repaying a loan is by <u>balloon repayments</u>.

A floating charge is on the <u>current assets</u> of the business.

A covenant in a loan agreement is <u>obligations on the receiver of the loan</u>.

When investing funds as a general rule risk and return are related: the higher the risk of an investment, the <u>higher</u> will be its anticipated return.

Task 2.5

Certificates of deposit	IOUs issued by large companies which can be either held to maturity or sold to third parties before maturity
Commercial paper	£50,000 or more for a fixed term which can be sold earlier than maturity
Gilts	Marketable British Government securities
Local authority stocks	Marketable securities with a slightly higher yield than government stocks
Bill of exchange	Unconditional order in writing from one person to another

Task 2.6

(a)

	Arrangement fee £	Loan interest £	Overdraft interest £	Total cost £
Option 1	4,060	27,840		31,900
Option 2		25,000	2,917	27,917
Option 3	2,500	30,000	2,917	35,417

(b)

Option 1	
Option 2	
Option 3	✓
None of the options	

PRACTICE ASSESSMENT 3
CASH MANAGEMENT

Time allowed: 2 hours

Cash Management Practice Assessment 3

Task 1.1

(a) **Which of the following is not a liquid asset?**

A   Inventory (stock)

B   Cash held in a deposit account

C   Cash held in a current account

D   Short-term investments

(b) A business has an average inventory (stock) holding period of 43 days, receives payment from its customers in 35 days and pays its suppliers in 55 days.

What is the cash operating cycle in days for the business?

A   133 days
B   63 days
C   47 days
D   23 days

(c) Given below is information on the working capital of a business.

	Days
Inventory (stock) turnover	21
Receivables' (debtors') payment period	35
Payables' (creditors') payment period	16

Which of the following statements is true?

A   The cash operating cycle of the business is 72 days.

B   The cash operating cycle of the business can be improved by reducing the credit terms available to customers from 30 days to 14 days.

C   Increasing the payables' (creditors') payment period will worsen the cash operating cycle of the business.

D   The cash operating cycle of the business is 30 days.

Task 1.2

There are many different types of cash flows.

Complete the table below by entering the correct description to match the type of cash receipt or cash payment.

Transaction	Type of receipt or payment
Sales receipts from customers	
Drawings	
Purchase of non-current (fixed) assets	
Receipt of insurance claim for damaged inventory (stock)	
Payment of wages	
Machine breakdown repair cost	

Regular
Irregular
Capital
Exceptional

Task 1.3

Mullins Ltd is a wholesaler who buys in its product and then sells the majority to the retail trade on credit but a small amount in its own shop for cash. Mullins Ltd is currently preparing its cash budget for the three months to June 20X6.

Sales to the retail trade are expected to be 120,000 units in April, 125,000 in May and 130,000 in June. In addition, it is expected that there will be sales of 5,000 units from the retail shop in each of the next three months.

A unit of the product will be sold to the retail trade at £1.65. Sales made from the retail shop will be made at £3 each for cash.

(a) **Complete the following table to calculate the value of both cash sales and retail sales for the three months ending in June 20X6.**

	April	May	June
	Units	Units	Units
Retail sales			
Cash sales			
	£	£	£
Retail sales			
Cash sales			

For budgetary purposes the assumption is that 30% of retail trade customers pay one month after the date of sale and 70% pay two months after the date of sale.

It is assumed that the receivables (debtors) at 31 March will pay as follows.

	£
In April	200,000
In May	180,000
	380,000

(b) **Complete the table below to calculate the cash receipts from sales for the three months ending in June.**

	Workings	April	May	June
		£	£	£
Cash sales				
Opening receivables (debtors)				
April sales				
May sales				
Total receipts from sales				

Task 1.4

Lucent Ltd is a candle maker and is preparing its cash budget for the three months ending June 20X6.

Production is expected to be 130,000 candles in April, 135,000 candles in May and 140,000 candles in June.

There is one unit of raw materials for each candle and there are currently 100,000 units of raw materials in the warehouse and it is intended to maintain inventory (stock) at this level.

The cost of raw materials for each candle is 60 pence. No price increase is expected in the budgetary period. All purchases are made in the month of production but not paid for until the following month. At 31 March 20X6 the payable (creditor) for purchases made during March was £120,000.

(a) **Complete the table below to determine the raw materials purchases budget in both units and £ for each of the three months ending in June.**

	Workings	April	May	June
		Units	Units	Units
Production				
Opening inventory (stock)				
Closing inventory (stock)				
Purchases in units				
		£	£	£
Purchases in £				

(b) **Complete the table below to show the payments to suppliers for each of the three months ending in June.**

	Workings	April	May	June
		£	£	£
Opening payables (creditors)				
April purchases				
May purchases				

Each candle takes six minutes of labour time to manufacture and production staff are paid £5 per hour. Wages are paid in the month in which they are incurred.

(c) **Complete the table below to determine the labour budget**.

	Workings	April	May	June
		£	£	£
April				
May				
June				

Task 1.5

The cash budget for Speights Ltd for the three months ended June has been partially completed. The following information is to be incorporated and the cash budget completed.

- Fixed production overheads are £25,000 per month. This includes depreciation of £5,000.

- Sales department costs are expected to be fixed at £12,000 per month including depreciation of £500 per month.

- The costs for the Speights Ltd's retail shop are fixed and are £7,000 per month including depreciation of £800.

- Administration overheads should be budgeted to be £25,000 each month.

- Overdraft interest is charged by the bank each month and should be budgeted at the rate of 1% per month on the overdrawn balance at the end of the previous month.

- All of the above costs are paid for in the month that they were incurred.

Using the additional information above, complete the cash budget for Speights Ltd for the three months ending in June. Cash inflows should be entered as positive figures and cash outflows as negative figures. Zeroes must be entered where appropriate to achieve full marks.

	April	May	June
	£	£	£
Receipts			
Total receipts – sales receipts	205,000	222,600	225,885
Payments			
Payments to suppliers	−110,000	−66,000	−86,000
Payments for wages	−62,000	−57,500	−72,000
Fixed production overhead			
Sales department costs			
Shop costs			
Administration overheads			
Overdraft interest			
Total payments			
Net cash flow			
Bank balance b/f	−220,000		
Bank balance c/f			

Task 1.6

(a) A business has been carrying out time series analysis on its sales volumes for the last three years. It wishes to use this time series analysis to forecast sales volumes for April, May and June 20X6.

The trend has been discovered to be a monthly increase of 20 units. In March 20X6 the trend figure for sales volume was 2,040 units. The time series analysis has also identified the following seasonal variations for months involved:

April	+43 units
May	+10 units
June	−25 units

The selling price of the unit is £12.

Monthly purchases are on average 60% of the value of sales.

Using the trend and monthly variations complete the table below to forecast the sales volume, sales value and purchases value for April, May and June 20X6.

	Forecast trend	Variation	Forecast sales volume	Forecast sales £	Forecast purchases £
April					
May					
June					

Additional information

As well as time series analysis the business tries to forecast wages costs for each period using an industry average wage rate index. The wages cost in March 20X6 was £10,200 when the wage rate index stood at 121. The forecast wage rate index for the next three months is as follows:

April	125
May	130
June	137

(b) What will be the forecast wages cost for each of the months of April, May and June 20X6?

Month	Wages cost £
April	
May	
June	

Task 2.1

The quarterly budget and actual figures for an organisation are provided below:

	Budgeted	Actual
	£	£
Cash sales	22,500	28,600
Receipts from credit customers	104,000	98,760
Cash purchases	(10,800)	(7,400)
Payments to credit suppliers	(54,700)	(61,200)
Wages and salaries	(25,600)	(30,200)
General expenses	(24,600)	(20,300)
Capital expenditure	0	(20,000)
Net cash flows	10,800	(11,740)
Opening balance	2,500	2,500
Closing balance	13,300	(9,240)

Prepare a reconciliation of budgeted cash flow with actual cash flow for the quarter. Highlight the appropriate description for each entry.

	£
Budgeted closing cash balance	
Surplus/shortfall in cash sales	
Surplus/shortfall in receipts from credit customers	
Increase/decrease in cash payments	
Increase/decrease in payments to credit suppliers	
Increase/decrease in wages and salaries	
Increase/decrease in general expenses	
Increase/decrease in capital expenditure	
Actual cash balance	

Task 2.2

Match each of the differences between budget and actual listed on the left with a possible cause of that difference from the list on the right.

| Surplus of cash sales |

Unexpected breakdown of necessary machinery which cannot be repaired

| Shortfall in receipts from credit customers |

Lower price offered for immediate receipt of cash

| Increase in payments to credit suppliers |

Sales being made for cash rather than on credit

| Increase in capital expenditure |

Payments to suppliers being made earlier

Task 2.3

Match each cause of a variance listed on the left with a possible course of action from the list on the right.

| Customers are taking longer to pay |

Reduce overtime working

| Capital expenditure which has not been budgeted for is being incurred |

Improve credit control

| Labour costs have increased |

Consider advertising campaign

| Sales volume has decreased |

Improve budgeting procedures

Task 2.4

Selecting from the picklists, complete the following sentences.

An overdraft will tend to have a [higher/lower]rate of interest than a bank loan. The interest will be charged on [the entire overdraft facility/the amount of the facility used]. An overdraft is [available for as long as required/repayable on demand] and is particularly useful for funding [capital expenditure/working capital].

A bank loan [will require/may require] covenants attached to it. A bank loan [will require/may require] a charge on the assets of the business. A floating charge is a charge on the [non-current (fixed) assets/current assets]. Repayment of a bank loan is [on demand/as negotiated]. A bank loan should be matched with [the income from the assets it finances/the working capital requirements].

Task 2.5

A business is considering an expansion project and has been looking into financing options for this project. One option is a bank loan of £400,000 with an initial facility fee of 0.5% of the loan amount and annual interest fixed at 6.5%. In order to fund the working capital required for the expansion the bank has also agreed an overdraft facility of £50,000 with an annual interest rate of 11%. The owners of the business believe that the average amount of the overdraft facility that will be used is £30,000 and this will only be for the last six months of the year.

What is the total cost of this financing arrangement for the first year?

A   £31,300
B   £29,650
C   £33,500
D   £30,750

Task 2.6

A company has produced a cash budget and believes that it will have £100,000 to invest in one month's time. The hope is that the money will be available for investment but it is possible that it will be required in two months' time. The finance director has identified four possible investment options:

Option 1	Investment in a fixed rate bank deposit account with an interest rate of 3% per annum. This account has a 30-day notice period.
Option 2	Investment in a variable rate bank deposit account with interest rate at 3% above base rate. This account has a 60-day notice period. The base rate expected in one month's time is 0.6%.
Option 3	Investment in 3.4% Treasury Stock 20X9 expected to be trading at £103.80 in one month's time.
Option 4	Investment in the shares of another company which according to analysts information should be trading at 140 pence in one month's time and whose share price should increase by 7% over the next year.

The company's treasury policy for investment is as follows:

- Return on investments should be maximised whenever possible.
- Risk should be minimised – investments should be categorised as low risk or high risk.
- Liquidity is of the highest importance.

(a) **Complete the table below on the basis that the cash will be needed in two months' time (ie one month after the investment is made).**

	Annual Return %	Risk – high/low	Liquidity acceptable?
Option 1			
Option 2			
Option 3			
Option 4			

(b) **Complete the table below on the basis that the cash will be needed in three months' time (ie two months after the investment is made).**

	Annual Return %	Risk – high/low	Liquidity acceptable?
Option 1			
Option 2			
Option 3			
Option 4			

(c) **Complete the table below showing which investment would be preferable under situations (a) and (b) according to the company's treasury policy.**

	Situation (a)	Situation (b)
Option 1		
Option 2		
Option 3		
Option 4		

(d) If the base rate were to fall this could affect both the interest rate from an investment or its capital value.

Complete the two tables below concerning interest rate and capital value for Options 1,2 and 3.

Interest rate

	Increase	Decrease	Remain the same
Option 1			
Option 2			
Option 3			

Capital value

	Increase	Decrease	Remain the same
Option 1			
Option 2			
Option 3			

PRACTICE ASSESSMENT 3
CASH MANAGEMENT

ANSWERS

Cash Management Practice Assessment 3 – Answers

Task 1.1

(a) A

(b) D

The cash operating cycle of the business is 43 + 35 − 55 = 23 days.

(c) B

Task 1.2

Transaction	Type of receipt or payment
Sales receipts from customers	Regular
Drawings	Capital
Purchase of non-current (fixed) assets	Irregular
Receipt of insurance claim for damaged inventory (stock)	Exceptional
Payment of wages	Regular
Machine breakdown repair cost	Irregular

Task 1.3

(a)

	April	May	June
	Units	Units	Units
Retail sales	120,000	125,000	130,000
Cash sales	5,000	5,000	5,000
	£	£	£
Retail sales (Units × £1.65)	198,000	206,250	214,500
Cash sales (Units × £3)	15,000	15,000	15,000

(b)

	Workings	April	May	June
		£	£	£
Cash sales		15,000	15,000	15,000
Opening receivables (debtors)		200,000	180,000	
April sales	198,000 × 30%		59,400	
	198,000 × 70%			138,600
May sales	206,250 × 30%			61,875
Total receipts from sales		**215,000**	**254,400**	**215,475**

Task 1.4

(a) Purchases budget

	Workings	April	May	June
		Units	Units	Units
Production		130,000	135,000	140,000
Opening inventory (stock)		(100,000)	(100,000)	(100,000)
Closing inventory (stock)		100,000	100,000	100,000
Purchases in units		**130,000**	**135,000**	**140,000**
		£	£	£
Purchases in £ (units × £0.60)		**78,000**	**81,000**	**84,000**

(b) Payments to suppliers

	Workings	April	May	June
		£	£	£
Opening payables (creditors)		120,000		
April purchases			78,000	
May purchases				81,000

(c) Labour budget

		April	May	June
		£	£	£
April	130,000/10 × £5	65,000		
May	135,000/10 × £5		67,500	
June	140,000/10 × £5			70,000

Task 1.5

Cash budget for the three months ended 30 June 20X6

	April	May	June
	£	£	£
Receipts			
Total receipts – sales receipts	205,000	222,600	225,885
Payments			
Payments to suppliers	−110,000	−66,000	−86,000
Payments for wages	−62,000	−57,500	−72,000
Fixed production overhead	−20,000	−20,000	−20,000
Sales department costs	−11,500	−11,500	−11,500
Shop costs	−6,200	−6,200	−6,200
Administration overheads	−25,000	−25,000	−25,000
Overdraft interest	−2,200	−2,519	−2,180
Total payments	−236,900	−188,719	−222,880
Net cash flow	−31,900	33,881	3,005
Bank balance b/f	−220,000	−251,900	−218,019
Bank balance c/f	−251,900	−218,019	−215,014

Task 1.6

(a)

	Forecast trend	Variation	Forecast sales volume	Forecast sales £	Forecast purchases £
April	2,060	+43	2,103	25,236	15,142
May	2,080	+10	2,090	25,080	15,048
June	2,100	−25	2,075	24,900	14,940

(b)

Month	Wages cost £
April 10,200 × 125/121	10,537
May 10,200 × 130/121	10,959
June 10,200 × 137/121	11,549

Task 2.1

	£
Budgeted closing cash balance	13,300
Surplus in cash sales	6,100
Shortfall in receipts from credit customers	(5,240)
Decrease in cash payments	3,400
Increase in payments to credit suppliers	(6,500)
Increase in wages and salaries	(4,600)
Decrease in general expenses	4,300
Increase in capital expenditure	(20,000)
Actual cash balance	**(9,240)**

Task 2.2

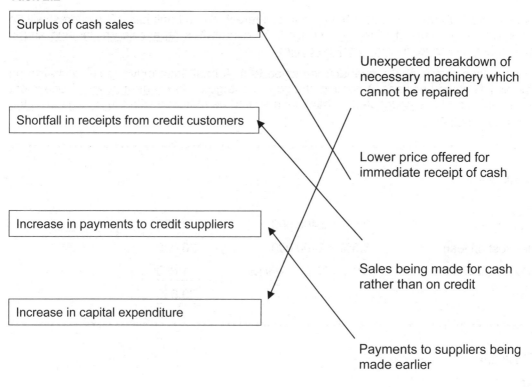

Task 2.3

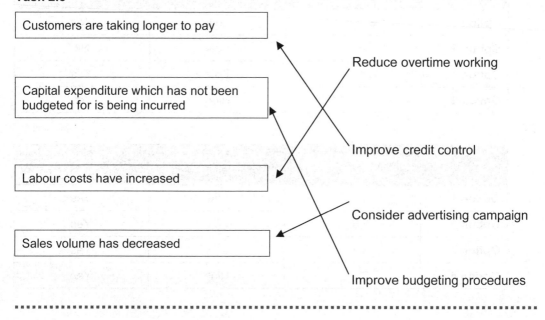

Task 2.4

An overdraft will tend to have a <u>higher</u> rate of interest than a bank loan. The interest will be charged on <u>the amount of the facility used</u>. An overdraft is <u>repayable on demand</u> and is particularly useful for funding <u>working capital</u>.

A bank loan <u>may require</u> covenants attached to it. A bank loan <u>may require</u> a charge on the assets of the business. A floating charge is a charge on the <u>current assets</u>. Repayment of a bank loan is <u>as negotiated</u>. A bank loan should be matched with <u>the income from the assets it finances</u>.

Task 2.5

B

Facility fee	0.5% × £400,000	2,000
Interest on loan	6.5% × £400,000	26,000
Overdraft interest	11% × 30,000 x 6/12	1,650
		29,650

Task 2.6

(a)

	Annual Return %	Risk – high/low	Liquidity acceptable?
Option 1	3	Low	Yes
Option 2	3.6	Low	No
Option 3	3.4	Low	Yes
Option 4	7	High	Yes

(b)

	Annual Return %	Risk – high/low	Liquidity acceptable?
Option 1	3	Low	Yes
Option 2	3.6	Low	Yes
Option 3	3.4	Low	Yes
Option 4	7	High	Yes

(c)

	Situation (a)	Situation (b)
Option 1		
Option 2		✓
Option 3	✓	
Option 4		

(d) **Interest rate**

	Increase	Decrease	Remain the same
Option 1			✓
Option 2		✓	
Option 3			✓

Capital value

	Increase	Decrease	Remain the same
Option 1			✓
Option 2			✓
Option 3	✓		

As interest rates generally fall the price (capital value) of gilts will increase so that the interest (which is fixed) falls to that of general interest rates.

PRACTICE ASSESSMENT 4
CASH MANAGEMENT

Time allowed: 2 hours

Cash Management Practice Assessment 4

Section 1

Task 1.1

(a) **Which one of the following equations best describes the cash operating cycle?**

A   average inventory (stock) turnover period + average payables' (creditors') payment period - average receivables' (debtors') collection period

B   average inventory (stock) turnover period + average receivables' (debtors') collection period - average payables' (creditors') payment period

C   average cash balance + average receivables' (debtors') collection period – average payables' (creditors') payment period

D   average cash balance – average receivables' (debtors') collection period + average payables' (creditors') payment period

(b) **Which of the following should a business do in order to improve its cash operating cycle?**

A   Increase inventories (stock) of raw material
B   Decrease the credit period taken from trade suppliers
C   Extend the credit period for customers
D   Reduce the time taken to produce its product

(c) A company's current cash operating cycle is 34 days.

Which of the following will have the effect of reducing the cash operating cycle?

A   Increasing the inventory (stock) turnover period by 3 days

B   Decreasing the payables' (creditors') payment period by 5 days

C   Decreasing the receivables' (debtors') collection period by 2 days

D   Increasing the average cash balance by 10%

••

Task 1.2

(a) **Which one of the following would be appropriate if a cash budget identified a short-term cash deficit?**

A   Replace non-current (fixed) assets
B   Issue shares
C   Implement better credit control procedures
D   Pay suppliers early

(b) **A company's cash budget highlights a short-term surplus in the future. Which of the following actions is least likely to be an appropriate use of the surplus?**

    A   Increase inventories (stock) and receivables (debtors) to improve customer service

    B   Invest in a short term deposit account

    C   Buy back the company's shares

    D   Reduce payables (creditors) by taking advantage of early settlement discounts from suppliers

Task 1.3

(a) You are given an extract from a company's records about the average hourly wage rate.

Complete the table to show the wage rate index for each month.

	Actual hourly wage rate	Wage rate Index
January	£6.00	100
February	£6.36	
March	£6.48	
April	£6.72	
May	£6.72	
June	£6.84	

Task 1.3

(b) Each unit of product requires 3 hours of labour and the production budget for July is to manufacture 12,500 units.

If the index for July is 115 what is the budgeted payment for labour hours?

Payment for July labour hours	£

Task 1.4

A company is budgeting its payments for purchases for the three months from July to September.

Production was 55,000 units in June and is expected to be 60,000 units in July, 70,000 units in August, and 65,000 units in each of September and October.

Each unit of product requires 2kg material which currently costs £6/kg. The unit price will increase to £6.30/kg on 1 September.

Suppliers are paid in the month following purchase. It is company policy to hold enough raw material in stock to meet 10% of the following month's production requirements.

(a) Complete the table below to calculate the purchases budget for the months from June to September and enter the month in which the cash payment is made to the suppliers.

	June	July	August	September
Production budget (units)				
Materials required for production (x 2kg)				
Less Opening inventory (stock) of raw materials				
Add Closing inventory (stock) of raw materials				
Purchases in kg				
Price per kg				
Cost of material purchases (£)				
Month in which cash paid to suppliers				

(b) With effect from 1 July, some of the suppliers have offered a 3% discount if payment is made within the month of purchase. Complete the table below to show the new payments for purchases for the months from July to September, assuming that the discount is available for 40% of purchases.

Cash paid to suppliers	Workings	July £	August £	September £
June purchases				
July purchases				
August purchases				
September purchases				
Total payments for purchases				

....

Task 1.5

The trend figures for sales in £ for a business for the four quarters of last year and the seasonal variations are estimated as:

	Trend sales £	Seasonal variations
Quarter 1	160,000	+11,200
Quarter 2	164,500	+14,805
Quarter 3	169,000	-5,070
Quarter 4	173,500	-22,555

(a) **Assuming the trend continues, complete the table to show the forecast sales for each of the four quarters of next year.**

	This years trend sales £	Additive adjustment for seasonal variation	Sales budget
Quarter 1			
Quarter 2			
Quarter 3			
Quarter 4			

(b) Cash from sales is received as follows:

40% in the quarter
55% in the following quarter
5% bad debts

What is the budgeted cash to be received from customers in quarter 4 (to the nearest £)?

A   67,578
B   165,692
C   100,062
D   167,640

Task 1.6

A company has completed its cash flow budget for the three months ending 31 March 20X9.

	January £	February £	March £
Total receipts	445,600	604,278	848,811
Total payments	(577,800)	(1,061,000)	(815,400)
Net cash flow	(132,200)	(456,722)	33,411
Cash balance b/f	560,000	427,800	(28,922)
Cash balance c/f	427,800	(28,922)	4,489

Unfortunately the company has forgotten to take account of bank interest when preparing the budget.

Interest is payable at 2% per month on any overdraft balance and the company receives 1% interest per month on any positive cash balance. Interest for the month is calculated on the cash balance held at the start of that month.

Complete the table below to reflect the interest and to show the new cash balances (round interest calculations to the nearest £)

Cash balance b/f	560,000		
Net cash flow	(132,200)	(456,722)	33,411
Interest – January			
Interest – February			
Interest – March			
Cash balance c/f			

Section 2

Task 2.1

The quarterly budget and actual figures for an organisation are provided below.

Complete the table to show the variance arising and use a + or − to indicate whether it is favourable or adverse.

	Budgeted cash flows	Actual cash flows	Variance
	£	£	£
Cash sales	32,500	28,600	
Receipts from credit customers	234,000	198,760	
Sale of machinery	0	7,500	
Payments to credit suppliers	(124,700)	(91,200)	
Wages and salaries	(35,600)	(30,200)	
General expenses	(14,600)	(10,300)	
Capital expenditure	0	(20,000)	
Drawings	(30,000)	(35,000)	
Net cash flows	61,600	48,160	
Opening balance	32,500	32,500	
Closing balance	94,100	80,660	

Task 2.2

Match the cause of a variance listed on the left with the list on the right of the possible impact that it may have on the cash budget.

Some customers, who previously bought goods on credit, are taking advantage of lower prices offered on cash sales

Increased payments for wages

A machine needed to be replaced unexpectedly when it broke down

Reduction in payments to suppliers

Material costs have decreased

sales

Reduction in receipts from credit

Large orders necessitated additional overtime working

Increased capital expenditure

Task 2.3

(a) **Using the list below, complete the table by inserting the correct explanations for each of the terms on the left**

Financial Term	Explanation
Covenant	
Hardcore overdraft	
Floating charge	
Fixed interest	

The maximum amount that a business can borrow in the form of an overdraft

Obligation or restriction placed on loan by loan provider

An overdraft which has effectively become part of the capital of the business

The return that the investor receives on an investment in gilts

Security that relates to a specific asset

Interest rate that is calculated by adding a margin to bank base rate

Security that relates to a group of assets that are constantly changing

Interest rate that is set at a constant rate for the duration of the borrowing.

(b) The directors of a company are forecasting increased sales opportunities and wish to purchase a new machine at a cost of £300,000. They will also require additional working capital of £80,000.

What would normally be the best method of financing these two elements of the expansion?

	Machine	Working capital
A	Bank loan	Overdraft
B	Overdraft	Bank loan
C	Overdraft	Overdraft
D	Bank loan	Bank loan

Task 2.4

A business needs help deciding whether or not to introduce a prompt payment discount in order to collect cash from its credit customers in sooner.

The sales budget is as follows:

	£
Period 1 sales	144,000
Period 2 sales	151,500
Period 3 sales	145,450
Period 4 sales	139,000
Period 5 sales	162,300

The original cash receipts budget was prepared assuming that 60% of sales were paid for by customers in the month following the sale and the remaining 37% of customers paid two months after the sale, with 3% of all debts remaining uncollected.

	Period 3 £	Period 4 £	Period 5 £
Period 1 sales £144,000 × 37%	53,280		
Period 2 sales £151,500 × 60%	90,900		
Period 2 sales £151,500 × 37%		56,055	
Period 3 sales £145,450 × 60%		87,270	
Period 3 sales £145,450 × 37%			53,817
Period 4 sales £139,000 × 60%			83,400
Total receipts from customers	**144,180**	**143,325**	**137,217**

The company is considering introducing a settlement discount at the start of period 3. The discount will be 2% for payments made in the month of the sale. This policy is expected to result in 40% of customers paying in the month of the sale, 30% paying in the month following the sale and the remaining 30% paying two months following the sale. As cash is being collected faster, the company is expecting to eliminate bad debts. It also expects sales to increase by 5% from period 3 because more customers will be attracted by the change in credit policy.

(a) **Complete the table below to calculate the forecast receipts from customers for each of periods 3, 4 and 5 if the system of settlement discounts is introduced**

	Workings	Period 3 £	Period 4 £	Period 5 £
Period 1 sales				
Period 2 sales				
Period 2 sales				
Period 3 sales				
Period 3 sales				
Period 3 sales				
Period 4 sales				
Period 4 sales				
Period 5 sales				
Total receipts from customers				

(b) **Complete the tables below to show the effects of introducing the discount system.**

	Period 3 £	Period 4 £	Period 5 £
Original receipts from customers			
Revised receipts from customers			
Overall increase/(decrease) in sales receipts			

Cost of prompt payment discount	Workings	Period 3 £	Period 4 £	Period 5 £
Period 3 sales				
Period 4 sales				
Period 5 sales				

Task 2.5

A company has produced a cash budget and believes that it will have £250,000 to invest in one month's time. The hope is that the money will be available for investment but it is possible that it will be required at some point within the next six months. The finance director has identified three possible investment options.

Option 1	Invest in shares in another company which, according to market information could be trading at 250 pence in one month's time and whose share price may increase by up to 7% over the forthcoming year.
Option 2	Invest in 4.0% Treasury Stock, redeemable in 5 year's time and expected to be trading at £107 in one month's time
Option 3	Invest in a bank deposit account which attracts interest at 3.5% above base rate and with a 3 month notice period. The base rate in one month's time is expected to be 1%

The company's treasury policy for investment is as follows:

- Return on investments should be maximised whenever possible.

- Risk should be minimised.

- Liquidity is of the highest importance.

(a) **Complete the table below, on the basis that the cash will be needed in three month's time (ie two months after the investment is made).**

	Annual Return %	Risk – high/low	Liquidity acceptable – Yes/No?
Option 1			
Option 2			
Option 3			

(b) **Use the information from the table you have completed to recommend which of the options, if any, should be selected**:

Given its treasury policy, the company should select [Option 1/Option 2/Option 3/ None of the options].

If however the cash will definitely not be required for at least six months, then the company should select [Option 1/Option 2/Option 3/ None of the options].

Task 2.6

(a) **Complete the table from the lists below by choosing the appropriate description and correctly matching the transactions to the type of payment.**

Type of payment	Description	Example transactions
Discretionary		
Non-discretionary		

Descriptions

Payments which can validly be cancelled or delayed

Payments which must be made on time for the business to continue

Transactions

PAYE and NI due to HM Revenue and Customs

Drawings

Training costs

Capital expenditure

Payment to credit suppliers

Annual loan interest

(b) **The following courses of action can be used by a business to manage cash balances.**

 (i) Finance capital expenditure differently eg bank loan

 (ii) Take advantage of prompt payment discount offered by suppliers

 (iii) Sell unutilised non-current (fixed) assets

 (iv) Buy materials in bulk to avoid price increases

 (v) Delay payment of dividends

Which of the actions listed above would help keep a company within its agreed overdraft limit?

A All of them
B (i), (ii), (iii), (v)
C (i), (iii), (v)
D (iii), (v)

PRACTICE ASSESSMENT 4
CASH MANAGEMENT

ANSWERS

Cash Management Practice Assessment 4 – Answers

Section 1

Task 1.1

(a) B

(b) D as this will reduce the inventory (stock) holding period

(c) C

Task 1.2

(a) C

(b) C

Task 1.3

(a)

	Actual hourly wage rate	Wage rate Index
January	£6.00	100
February	£6.36	106
March	£6.48	108
April	£6.72	112
May	£6.72	112
June	£6.84	114

(b)

Payment for July labour hours	£258,750 (12500 x 3 x £6.00 x 1.15)

Task 1.4

(a)

	June	July	August	September
Production budget (units)	55,000	60,000	70,000	65,000
Materials required for production (x 2kg)	110,000	120,000	140,000	130,000
Less Opening inventory (stock) of raw materials	(11,000)	(12,000)	(14,000)	(13,000)
Add Closing inventory (stock) of raw materials	12,000	14,000	13,000	(13,000)
Purchases in kg	111,000	122,000	139,000	130,000
Price per kg	£6	£6	£6	£6.30
Cost of material purchases (£)	£666,000	£732,000	£834,000	£819,000
Month in which cash paid to suppliers	July	August	September	October

(b)

Cash paid to suppliers	Workings	July £	August £	September £
June purchases		666,000		
July purchases	732,000×40%×97%	284,016		
	732,000×60%		439,200	
August purchases	834,000×40%×97%		323,592	
	834,000×60%			500,400
September purchases	819,000×40%×97%			317,772
Total payments for purchases		**£950,016**	**£762,792**	**£818,172**

Task 1.5

(a)

	This years trend sales £	Additive adjustment for seasonal variation	Sales budget
Quarter 1	178,000	+ 11,200	189,200
Quarter 2	182,500	+ 14,805	197,305
Quarter 3	187,000	−5,070	181,930
Quarter 4	191,500	−22,555	168,945

(b) D

(181,930 × 55% + 168,945 × 40%) = £167,640

Task 1.6

Cash balance b/f	560,000	433,400	(18,988)
Net cash flow	(132,200)	(456,722)	33,411
Interest – January (1% × 560,000)	5,600		
Interest – February (1% × 433,400)		4,334	
Interest – March (2% × 18,988)			(380)
Cash balance c/f	433,400	(18,988)	14,043

Section 2

Task 2.1

	Budgeted cash flows	Actual cash flows	Variance
	£	£	£
Cash sales	32,500	28,600	−3,900
Receipts from credit customers	234,000	198,760	−35,240
Sale of machinery	0	7,500	+7,500
Payments to credit suppliers	(124,700)	(91,200)	+33,500
Wages and salaries	(35,600)	(30,200)	+5,400
General expenses	(14,600)	(10,300)	+4,300
Capital expenditure	0	(20,000)	−20,000
Drawings	(30,000)	(35,000)	−5,000
Net cash flows	61,600	48,160	−13,440
Opening balance	32,500	32,500	0
Closing balance	94,100	80,660	−13,440

Task 2.2

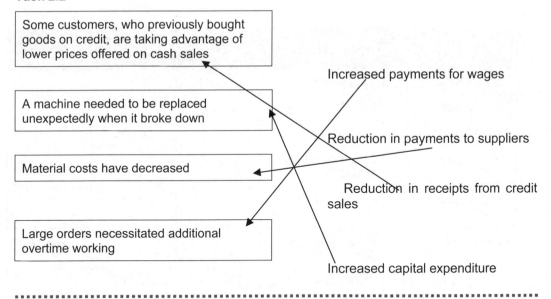

Some customers, who previously bought goods on credit, are taking advantage of lower prices offered on cash sales

A machine needed to be replaced unexpectedly when it broke down

Material costs have decreased

Large orders necessitated additional overtime working

Increased payments for wages

Reduction in payments to suppliers

Reduction in receipts from credit sales

Increased capital expenditure

Task 2.3

(a)

Financial Term	Explanation
Covenant	Obligation or restriction placed on loan by loan provider
Hardcore overdraft	An overdraft which has effectively become part of the capital of the business
Floating charge	Security that relates to a group of assets that are constantly changing
Fixed interest	Interest rate that is set at a constant rate for the duration of the borrowing

(b)   A

Task 2.4

(a)

	Workings	Period 3 £	Period 4 £	Period 5 £
Period 1 sales	£144,000 × 37%	53,280		
Period 2 sales	£151,500 × 60%	90,900		
Period 2 sales	£151,500 × 37%		56,055	
Period 3 sales	£145,450 × 1.05 × 40%x98%	59,867		
Period 3 sales	£145,450 × 1.05 × 30%		45,817	
Period 3 sales	£145,450 × 1.05 × 30%			45,817
Period 4 sales	£139,000 × 1.05 × 40%x98%		57,212	
Period 4 sales	£139,000 × 1.05 × 30%			43,785
Period 5 sales	£162,300 × 1.05 × 40%x98%			66,803
Total receipts from customers		**204,047**	**159,084**	**156,405**

(b)

	Period 3 £	Period 4 £	Period 5 £
Original receipts from customers	144,180	143,325	137,217
Revised receipts from customers	204,047	159,084	156,405
Overall increase/(decrease) in sales receipts	**+59,867**	**+15,759**	**+19,188**

Cost of prompt payment discount	Workings	Period 3 £	Period 4 £	Period 5 £
Period 3 sales	£145,450 × 1.05 × 40% × 2%	−1,222		
Period 4 sales	£139,000 × 1.05 × 40% × 2%		−1,168	
Period 5 sales	£162,300 × 1.05 × 40% × 2%			−1,363

Task 2.5

(a)

	Annual Return %	Risk – high/low	Liquidity acceptable-Yes/No
Option 1	7%	High	Yes
Option 2	3.7%	Low	Yes
Option 3	4.5%	Low	No

(b)   Given its treasury policy, the company should select Option 2.

If however the cash will definitely not be required for at least six months, then the company should select Option 3.

Task 2.6

(a)

Type of payment	Description	Example transactions
Discretionary	Payments which can validly be cancelled or delayed	Drawings Training costs Capital expenditure
Non-discretionary	Payments which must be made on time for the business to continue	PAYE and NI due to HM Revenue and Customs Payment to credit suppliers Annual loan interest

(b)   C

Notes

ANNIE L

ANNIE LENNOX

LUCIAN RANDALL

ORION

AN ORION PAPERBACK

This is a Carlton Book

First published in Great Britain in 1994 by Orion Books Ltd, Orion House,
5 Upper St Martin's Lane, London, WC2H 9EA.

Text and design © 1994 Carlton Books Ltd
CD Guide format © 1994 Carlton Books Ltd

A CIP catalogue record for this book is available from the British Library.

ISBN 1 85797 590 1

Edited, designed and typeset by Impact Editions
Printed in Italy

THE AUTHOR
Lucian Randall has worked for a variety of publications as a freelance journalist
based in London. He lives with a strange collection of music and a very old stereo.

CONTENTS

INTRODUCTION

Soulful and passionate or intense and contemplative. Annie Lennox—always unique.

Making an impression in the world of popular music has never been easy, especially for a woman. A star needs a fiercely individual personality, powerful voice and an inventive image, to be original without having to compromise. Annie Lennox is one of those rare people who has made full use of all those qualities.

She has cleared a path for the new breed of female artists around today—the outspoken 'Riot Grrrls', for example—in being a star who has always had the talent and tenacity to release records that sound so individual it can be difficult to believe the same person is involved in all of them. That's all part of the job that Annie Lennox has been doing for 16 years now. Her music is a rarity in pop—personal songs that are not afraid to explore darker emotions, but still manage to be catchy and tuneful enough to win an enormous base of fans.

Each song and each accompanying video is completely different: different costumes, different face, different mood; even her hair changes totally from appearance to appearance. One record might have a synthesizer-based feel, the next a rock sound and another will depend upon a percussion riff. Nothing is

experimentation is one of Annie Lennox's major strengths in competing with the faceless pop that swamps the charts: equally bold both as a solo artist and with long-time Eurythmics partner Dave Stewart.

"It's no mean feat to write a good song—it takes skill and courage," she once said of the work that goes into writing. "If you can put as much commitment into it and really believe in what you're doing, then you're being true to yourself."

From the early days of limited recognition in the late Seventies punk-inspired band The Tourists, through incredible success with Eurythmics in the Eighties, she has stuck to her convictions and vision even when those around her thought she had to be out of her senses. Her determination to be a respected artist would also make waves outside the narrow world of pop and influence contempory fashions.

At a time when 'gender-benders' such as Culture Club's make-up wearing frontman, Boy George, were redefining what was an acceptable appearance in society generally, she was becoming a role model for women and an icon for many gay people. Like Boy George, Annie's early years of colourful and exciting image changes pushed back boundaries, and other

certain until the singer looks into the camera, either directly or with a quick, piercing glance from those clear, knowing eyes. At the same time, that unmistakable, powerful, rock-soul voice cuts in. Then it's obvious. It càn only be Annie Lennox.

Her individuality could have condemned her to a career on the fringe of music, but instead it has become a trademark and an important contribution to her rise up the dizzy slopes of superstardom, a trail of inventive and powerful recordings behind her. Constant women in pop realized they could do more than just sing about happy love, smiling prettily.

That sort of recognition and responsibility is always difficult to deal with, but, with the passage of time and perhaps better adjusted to stardom, she has also involved herself with social and political issues.

And now she's a solo artist. After all the work she put into getting to the top, few would blame Annie for relaxing a little and producing formulaic pop. The reverse is true—she's more of an individual than ever, and the proof can be seen in the unconventional, faded prima donna look she adopted for 1992's *Diva* album.

Annie explained: "I've chosen the image of the diva who has seen better days, whose beauty is rather ruined—you can see the experience there." The cover shot could have been uncommercial. Annie doesn't make mistakes like that. It was a best seller.

It would be tempting to think that Annie Lennox can do no wrong, but her ride to the top has been far from easy, with more than a fair share of setbacks and tragedies, both professional and personal. Being a strong, female character, as well as an artist of originality, hasn't made things easier either. Any refusal to fit the mould of a pop bimbo inevitably makes some people feel threatened, and Annie has always been open to attack by the predatory tabloid press. They simply see this intensely private person as very fair game for scandal and gossip.

Such interest in Annie Lennox is not surprising. From the earliest days as a struggling musician in Seventies' London, through the years with Dave Stewart, her career has never been less than fascinating to follow. With her first solo album behind her, the creative output of this enigmatic and ground-breaking singer shows no sign of flagging, as she moves into a new decade with all the creativity and force which marks her out as a unique performer.

Major success came with 'Sweet Dreams...'

THE FLAUTIST WHO TURNED INTO A TOURIST

The truth is, Annie Lennox didn't want to be a pop star, with a musical portfolio packed full with an incredible number of hit singles, albums and awards. She wanted to be a classical flute player, or 'flautist'.

Attending London's Royal Academy of Music was the turning point for the young Scottish musician, who quickly felt frustrated by the constraints of formal classical training. "The atmosphere was Victorian, the teaching mediocre, and I felt out of it," she said later. A good thing as it turned out—society may have lost a talented classical musician, but it gained a classic pop singer who has had the world humming along to hits like 'Sweet Dreams (Are Made Of This)', 'Sisters Are Doin' It For Themselves', 'Angel', and plenty more.

Yet there is nothing in the formative years of Tom and Dorothy Lennox's talented, only child to suggest that she would one day rebel against convention to become a cross-dressing star and song writer. Far from

Annie developed her own style of performing on stage after leaving classical training.

it. She was born in Aberdeen on Christmas Day, 1954, her father a boiler-maker and her mother a cook. She spent the first few years of her life cramped, but happy, in a tenement apartment.

Early Promise

Annie showed an early interest in the creative arts—poetry, drawing and music, encouraged and supported by her parents (her father played bagpipes). Her talent for music was also recognized at Aberdeen High School for Girls where she learned piano, sang in a choir, and later made full use of an old flute in the school orchestra. She went on to play in symphony orchestras and military bands, as well as attending the dance classes of tutor Marguerite Feltges who introduced her pupils to a form of Greek dance known

Eurythmics would have a reputation for looking quirky, as well as sounding unusual.

as 'Eurhythmics'.

By the age of 14, playing classical music was competing for her attention with parties, boys and the exciting soul sound of Tamla Motown: The Supremes, Marvin Gaye, The Four Tops and the like. Like any teenager, Annie's developing personality often brought her into conflict with her parents.

"I suppose I was very headstrong—still am!—but I felt I was battling for my own existence," she said of her introduction to dancing and the soul music which was

> "Teachers at school would praise me for my 'talent' on the one hand and then on the other they'd be really cruel and sarcastic because I wasn't any good at maths."
> *Annie Lennox on being musical at school*

Dave appeared more manic than reflective to young Annie when the pair first met.

to be such an inspiration. She felt teenage troubles more intensely as an only child and something of a loner, her impressions reinforced by teachers' ambivalent responses to her abilities: "Teachers at school would praise me for my 'talent' on the one hand, and then on the other they'd be really cruel and sarcastic because I wasn't any good at maths. I developed a kind of dual superiority/inferiority personality complex."

Good at maths or not, she still won a place at London's prestigious Royal Academy of Music at the age of 17. Determined to support herself when she went away, she spent the Summer enduring the stench of a frozen fish factory to secure an income. In September 1971, she left Aberdeen for the bright lights of London. But it was a disappointment. Despite her love of classical music, the structure and formalized teaching saw Lennox depressed and frustrated for much of her three years at the Academy.

Classic Rebellion

Looking at the experience with characteristic Scottish earthiness, she later pointed out that at least she was provided with a catharsis which gave her the impetus to break free and express herself: "I have to thank the Academy for giving me the opportunity to rebel against it so violently," she recalled. "Because it subsequently led me to what I wanted to do. If I hadn't spent all those years practising and playing music, then I don't think I would ever have had the ability and courage to go for a career in rock." Never one to do things by halves, her violent rebellion took the form of leaving the Academy just weeks before her final exams.

She stuck it out in London for the next few years, rediscovering her love of pop and soul music in the record collections of friends, particularly struck by the work of singer/songwriter Joni Mitchell. Realizing she had a talent for writing and singing herself, she decided to be a waitress to pay her way while she concentrated on developing these abilities. But early forays into

covers in pubs, clubs and "Once even to the troops!" It was all good stuff in terms of acquainting Lennox with the harsh ways of the music business and she never forgot that she was definitely well out of that unpleasant world.

"There are thousands of no-hopers in those

performing, which included playing in a folksy band and a jazz-fusion band, seemed to be wrong directions for the young singer.

The furthest she went off course in those early years was to be paired up with another female singer, through a manager of dubious character, who christened them Stocking Tops. Even years later, this was still a source of embarrassment for Lennox when questioned in a magazine interview.

"Oh God, I wish I'd never mentioned that," she cringed. "I was very young, didn't know anything. It seemed the only way to get started." Not surprisingly the two only lasted for a few dead-end gigs, singing

Annie showcasing her early live energy, keyboard prowess, and plucked eyebrows.

The Tourists were to have some success—shortlived, but they enjoyed it while it lasted.

> "She was really the turning point, because she was someone I wanted to be all right for. When I met Annie I was about as far off as you could be into orbit. She was my saving grace."
> *Dave Stewart*

situations—still dreaming of stardom in some seedy, clapped-out pub doing Beatles and Simon and Garfunkel cover versions. God rest their weary heads!"

Meeting of minds

The break from the seedy circuit began for Annie Lennox while waitressing at Pippins Restaurant in Hampstead, north London. One evening in the Autumn of 1976, a friend brought along someone to meet Lennox: a rather hairy, dishevelled, out of work musician from Sunderland called Dave Stewart.

It could have been a more auspicious first meeting. Lennox's first impression of the man who would be her partner, emotionally for the next few years, and professionally for a decade and a half, was not promising: "I thought he was a complete nutter."

As a striking blonde singer, Annie would often be dubbed the British Debbie Harry.

That he was sporting a large fur-collared overcoat, Tony the Tiger sunglasses and bleeding from an ear which had recently been inexpertly pierced, possibly had something to do with this initial impression. Then

Annie was passionate where Peet Coombes was introspective—and the two didn't always gel well when sharing lead vocals .

24, he'd been around for some time in the music business and had come along to offer some advice. Like her, he had a long standing love affair with pop music, and was impressed with the 22-year-old Annie from the start.

"She has a different attitude," he later said. "She was fresh and I was immediately knocked out by her. I'd been taking LSD every day for a year. That sounds light-hearted, but when I look back on it I was really lucky not to end up the way most people did. She was

really the turning point, because she was someone I wanted to be all right for. When I met Annie I was about as far off as you could be into orbit. She was my saving grace."

Destined for music

The boy who would be half Eurythmics and a world-class producer/collaborator/friend to stars like Bob Dylan, Mick Jagger and Tom Petty, was born September 8, 1952. He was quite a sporty, mischievous lad, until a cartilage injury at 13 put him in hospital. There he relieved the boredom with a guitar. He continued to work on improving his playing at home, equally as influenced by soul and pop as young Annie, and unknowingly helped by his older brother.

"I used to sneak all his records out of his room, that's how I first learned the guitar properly. He had these compilation albums with all the Stax singles on them. He was nuts about them. I sat down with his guitar—which I used to borrow before he got home and

The organized Annie was to make a strange partner for laidback Dave Stewart. But amazingly, the duo worked well together.

rushed out to the garage with it—and copied everything note-for-note."

By 16, he'd left home for good (having had a narrow escape from teenage fame when Bell Records approached him to be the new David Cassidy!). He taught guitar to pay his way and played at medieval-style banquets in a castle before eventually teaming up with folksy Sunderland singer Brian Harrison. As Stewart and Harrison, they had some good fortune

which led to Dave's augmenting the duo in Autumn 1971 to a quartet, a pop-folk band called Longdancer. They enjoyed a certain success until they split up at the end of 1974. Dave, for one, had thought they should have been more modern.

"During this period, I was mad about T Rex. I

Critics weren't always kind, but The Tourists reckoned they'd have The Last Laugh.

> **"She's such a changeable person that you never know which one you're gonna deal with. You knock on the door one day and she says, 'Hi, come in, have a cup of tea'. Knock on the door the next day and she punches you on the nose."**
> *Dave on Annie's character!*

A fun and almost Swedish look for The Tourists' front woman on Top Of The Pops.

wanted us to do more over-the-top pop/electric things with more visually stimulating images. But I didn't explain myself very well, so everyone in the group just thought I was mad." Those ideas would see the light of day much later in Eurythmics.

Stewart started a downward spiral after Longdancer, touring round Europe with Sunderland mate Peet Coombes, taking too many drugs and staggering out of three car crashes. It was in 1976 that he set up a record shop in Kilburn, London, called Small Mercies, just before meeting Annie for the first time. Annie soon recovered from her original shock of meeting Stewart in the restaurant. He turned out to be a likable character, with a sense of humour. Once Annie performed a few of her songs to him, he

immediately felt he knew how they could be arranged in a band.

The two realized they had a lot in common both musically and personally, despite Dave being a pretty offbeat character in comparision with Annie—"Will you marry me?" was the very first thing he said to her. They soon moved into Annie's new, rundown

If The Tourists didn't work out, Annie could perhaps have had a career as a garden ornament. Dave doesn't seem convinced.

apartment together.

Their partnership led the press to speculate that Dave was a Svengali figure guiding Annie's career. True, he had more experience in the music business, but, at the same time, Annie had a lot of drive. She was very disciplined from her classical days. In reality, theirs was probably more of a genuine partnership than would make a good tabloid story.

Surviving

The going was tough to begin with, surviving and working in the semi-derelict apartment, using a friend's studio in the basement to play with ideas. Dave and Peet Coombes had been in contact with a publishing company run by Geoff Hannington and Olav Wyper, later to form Logo Records. Wyper and Hannington had been marketing chiefs at RCA Records in London and were now setting out on their own. At the time, Dave and Peet had some songs written, but had not

> "We were eager and enthusiastic about the songs. We felt like three gypsies on a mad adventure."
> *Annie Lennox on The Catch turning into The Tourists*

been able to make a demo because neither of them was a particularly good singer. Hannington and Wyper told them to come back when they had a singer.

The first deal

They came back with Annie. Wyper recalled afterwards how the three began performing their songs live for him in his office. He was not over impressed by the music, but was astounded by Annie's voice. He rushed next door to get Hannington saying: "I think we've really

Just another band? Forceful and poppy, The Tourists would still never make as much impact as Eurythmics.

found something here." This impromptu performance got them £300 (then $600) each, a publishing deal and later a rather unwise six-album contract which would tie them up and come back to haunt them until well into Eurythmics days. At the time though, they really needed the money.

The doors would eventually slide shut on The Tourists, Annie and Peet's musical differences were part of the problem.

With a contract and a name, The Catch, the three released a single in October 1977 which made absolutely no impact at all in most places, and is consequently now a rare collector's item. 'Borderline', penned by Annie, and the Coombes/Stewart B-side, 'Black Blood', was a minor hit in Holland, but by that time the band had decided to add a couple of new members and alter their name and image, changes that were greeted by their label with some confusion and disapproval.

But there was nowhere for the band to go as The Catch. Two session musicians who had been drafted in to gig with them had departed, leaving the other three on their own, but still excited by the possibilities of the band.

"We were eager and enthusiastic about the songs," said Annie. "We felt like three gypsies on a mad adventure." The gypsies added to the band with drummer Jim 'do it' Toomey (who'd played with Colin Blunstone and helped them gig as The Catch) and Eddie Chin, a Maylasian-born bassist with a silly moustache whose real name was Yung Fook Chin. Their first gig was at the Hope and Anchor in Islington, London, where Eddie read off a chord sheet at his feet

A band left on the shelf. From left, Dave Stewart, Annie Lennox, Peet Combes, Jim 'do it' Toomey and Eddie Chin.

as he played.

"We never spent too much time on rehearsals. We work out basically what's required and everyone puts their own ideas into it. And if we're pleased with what's come out—right, we'll try it on stage," explained Annie.

Tourists on show

A new look needed a new name. The Spheres of Celestial Influence was briefly toyed with and would much later make a reappearance as a pseudonym for Annie and Dave on the B-side of Annie's duet with Al

Eye-catching costumes and a drum-stick. What more does a young singer need?

hard-core punks felt themselves to be very 'real'. This wasn't good news for anyone who came over as 'impostors', and Annie's dayglo outfits and peroxide hair, coupled with power-poppy songs, ensured that the band took plenty of flak and hostility from the black-clad bondage brigade.

Despite this, The Tourists built up a reputation and following with exciting live performances. The rather introspective Peet Coombes took care of most lyric writing and singing duties, his serious style and obscure songs a contrast to Annie's energy.

"You could say that we're trying to use our music

Green. Eventually, a bus ride past an Information Centre solved titular problems for their punky sort of new band. They decided that they would call themselves The Tourists.

The fledgling band suffered from the aggression of the British punk scene of the later Seventies, where

The Annie Lennox patented unnerving stare in the early stages of development.

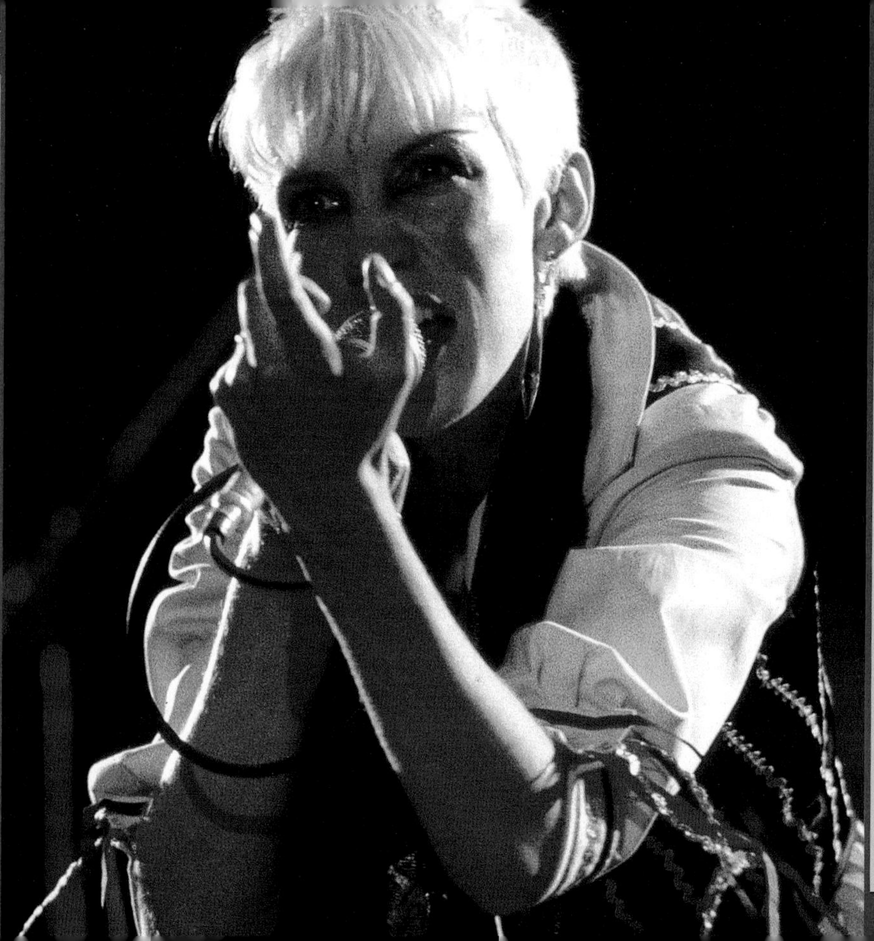

CHAPTER 1: THE FLAUTIST WHO TURNED INTO A TOURIST

and our act to offer some kind of reassurance to people who're anxious but afraid to step outside conventional barriers," Annie commented at the time.

Despite the success, there was quite a problem convincing Logo to let them release their new-style material on vinyl—Logo had rather hoped they would follow the craze for disco. "It was incredible," remembered Annie with some amazement. "We were playing every night to packed venues yet the record company wouldn't release our material."

The struggle for success

They only got the green light after much negotiation between The Tourists' managers, Arnakata, and Logo. All the fuss had been over the first, eponymous album of June 1979, recorded in Cologne, Germany, with producer Conny Plank, who'd also worked with Ultravox and German electro-pioneers Can. It was a power-poppy effort, more enthusiastic than professional sounding, which found no warm reception with the press—seemingly, the recording engineer just hadn't captured the live feel.

The album spawned two singles, both written by Coombes, at times sounding like a power pop version of Bob Dylan—'Blind Among The Flowers' and 'The Loneliest Man In The World'. Neither of his quirky songs did much to the charts, although 'Blind' was a

The Tourists had been fun in parts, but the experience would exhaust Dave and Annie.

landmark in that it was the first ever Dave Stewart production, and the album occasionally showed flashes of the sparsity that would define Eurythmics.

The Tourists were best in the flesh, as was proved by a successful first national tour late in 1979 supporting Roxy Music. It wasn't until singles from October's *Reality Effect* were released, that The Tourists were really launched on record. On this second album, Annie played keyboards and shared

lead vocals with Peet, resulting in a similar feel to the first album, heavy on the power chords. Here there was greater depth though, the band having experimented with odd atmospheric sounds and even an Eastern strings feel to one track.

A Dusty hit

The second album was more favourably received by the music critics. Weekly rock paper *Sounds* commented: "They've got just the right amount of suss to utilise their talents to generate quite surprising quantities of agreeable sensations." From that second album came their Blondie-esque, 'fun' cover of the

Contrary to popular belief, Dave was not—musically—just a figure in the background.

Dusty Springfield hit 'I Only Want To Be With You' which zoomed up the British charts to Number 4, resulting in a performance on British TV's *Top Of The Pops*. In the USA, the single only hit Number 83.

The follow-up, from the same album, was called 'So Good To Be Back Home', and bore more than a slight resemblance to 'I Only Wanna Be With You', particularly with lines like "Only one thing I wanna do/I wanna get back home to you". It zipped up to Number 8 in the UK in February 1980, promoted with a 14-city British tour that culminated at London's Hammersmith Odeon (now the Hammersmith Apollo). In a jibe at the music press, who were by then quite unfriendly, the tour was entitled The Last Laugh. It was a reflection of the strain from the constant critical bombardment the band were receiving, for the music, the lineup and Annie's image.

"I do this sort of thing because it gets the name of the band across. Unfortunately, the general media are so repressive, always exploiting a woman's sex, looking for an angle like 'When are you and Dave going to get married?'" she told weekly music paper *Melody Maker* in early 1980. "I try and steer them onto another tack... but sometimes it gets depressing.

"However, I'm sure rock journalists yawn every time they hear a girl singer saying that she's looked on as one of the boys in the band. But the reason girls feel obliged to say that is because the mass media is so obsessed with keeping a woman 'in her place'. Sometimes I don't know which is worse—that, or music papers accusing me of trying to come on like the next Debbie Harry... which is absurd."

Stuck with the Sixties

The Tourists had made some impact, though, and Annie received a Scotstar from the Scottish music industry in recognition of their achievements. But 'So Good...' was to be their last hit. It became obvious, through increasingly unfavourable press, that covering a Dusty song had labelled them as Sixties-philes and done the band more harm than good in a music scene still besotted with Punk and New Wave. 'So Good...' didn't chart at all in America, and a Lennox song wouldn't break in the States until 'Sweet Dreams...' came out.

"We rose to fame on a song that came out almost by accident," complained Annie with some justification. "We did it so casually at the time, but the press absolutely slaughtered us and you can only take a beating for so long—no one came to ask me what I felt like."

Still, as a result of their hits, the album *Reality*

When The Tourists split, the two would be left in the cold and up against the odds.

Effect did quite well, having actually gone platinum by the early Eighties. The band, however, was not doing so well at the turn of the decade. Annie and Dave felt they should be contributing more to the writing. As it was, Peet Coombes was doing the most, but wasn't really contributing in interviews: a difficult situation. Matters were not made any better by the worsening relationship with Logo Records, who the band wanted to leave. Logo eventually had to let them go to RCA, but only after much legal wrangling.

The new partnership began with a low-key 40-date tour of the USA, travelling in Dolly Parton's tour bus, which led to weighty questions for Dave: "We spent most of our time wondering how Dolly Parton fitted into any of the bunks because the space between the bunks and the roof of the bus was so narrow." At the tour's end, they flew to Montserrat to record what would prove to be their last album, with Annie once again singing in the breathy, punk-girl style she would dump once in Eurythmics.

Left in the basement

Released in November 1980, *Luminous Basement* features a rare Lennox-penned song, the ambient, sweetly menacing 'One Step Nearer The Edge'. Album three wasn't to be a big success with the public or critics, having a similar, light-but-ironic feel to it that had

> "We rose to fame on a song that came out almost by accident. We did it so casually at the time, but the press absolutely slaughtered us and you can only take a beating for so long."
> *Annie Lennox on 'I Only Want To Be With You'*

been evident on the first album and was so desperately untrendy in the early Eighties. Sounding like the cult English band XTC in some places, it was poorly received despite being backed by an ambitious, energetic "Luminous Tour" toward the end of the year, and a single, 'Don't Say I Told You So'. The band didn't give up though, embarking on a tour of Australia, Europe and the USA.

Sadly, though perhaps not surprisingly, they didn't get too far into the schedule. Feeling the strain of all the cumulative pressures, Annie collapsed on stage in Australia. Soon afterwards Peet Coombes left the band. They continued as a four-piece for a while, but it was inevitable that they would have to split up. This they did in early 1981.

Success and happiness were a long way off in the dark days of The Tourists' split.

"Our musical attitudes were becoming polarized, as well as having to cope with our steadily deteriorating personal relationships. I'm greatly relieved at the decision and glad it's all over, but it was fun while it lasted," Annie told the press. Peet Coombes' character, in particular, contrasted too much with those of the future Eurythmics.

"Peet was very influenced by The Byrds and that kind of sound—12-string guitars and things," recalled Dave, "which Annie and I liked—but we were more influenced by Tamla Motown and all the electronic things that were coming out of Germany." They would look for a new sort of sound in their next project.

We Tourists are one

Annie and Dave had drawn closer as a result of their experiences. They knew to a greater extent what they wanted musically and professionally—they had certainly found out what they didn't want—and they were left in the wreckage of The Tourists with just each other. Perhaps not just each other—there were also debts of £15,000 (then $30,000) to consider. But they had a new determination to work together, to put their musical ideas into practice and they had a feeling they could really succeed next time.

> "If you want to be in a pop group, you either become completely debauched and die of a drug overdose after a couple of years, or else you renounce everything and live like a nun. I think I've straddled them both."
> *Annie*

'EVERYBODY'S LOOKING FOR SOMETHING...'

The former Tourists were collectively written off by most of the music world, leaving Annie Lennox and Dave Stewart with a recording deal and not much else. Even their record company wasn't filled with enthusiasm at the thought of any other projects involving that girl singer and that strange, shaggy-haired guitarist.

If no-one else had any confidence, the two were still determined to make it, even as their personal relationship came under incredible strain. It became obvious that two such fiercely individual and creative spirits would have to end their emotional involvement if they were to continue with their music.

"The closer we got professionally, the more we needed our own space. We know each other exactly."

When Eurythmics got off the ground, Dave and Annie were only partners in music, their personal relationship sacrificed to success.

From behind the ruins of The Tourists, a new group was to emerge. And a new Annie.

outlined Dave. "It's like ESP and, for writing and recording, it can be fantastic." Eurythmics took precedence over everything else, Dave and Annie deciding to stay together professionally to continue with the music.

Demos with Conny

They went back to Conny Plank, the one-time Tourists producer in Germany, and did some demos that were slightly influenced by German electromeisters Kraftwerk and DAF. Plank was enthused by what the duo wanted to do, and saw the production and commercial potential in Annie, rather than just the girlie singer image the press had inflicted on her in the old band.

"I'm also a songwriter, I'm also part of an actress, part of a designer, part of a clothes designer," said Annie, refreshed by the new direction. "There are so many things that come into it and I feel it's so fulfilling." Their sessions were experimental, in a deliberate attempt to avoid the restraints of a fixed, constricting line-up. Help came in the shape of Holgar Czukay and Jaki Liebzeit from German experimental group Can, with DAF's Robert Gohl and Blondie's Clem Burke on drums.

The duo had a vision of a European, "alienating" element for their new sound.

> "Neither of us is a songwriter in the traditional sense... We like to create sound pictures. An idea is like a piece of clay, that you just play with until a shape starts to appear."
> *Annie*

The suspicions RCA harboured about the potential for success of this strange pair weren't put to rest when they were told that Dave and Annie were adopting the distinctly uncommercial sounding name of Eurythmics. According to Dave, the word (from the Greek dance Eurhythmics that Annie had learned as a kid) seemed to sum up both the "European and rhythmical" elements of this new band. He even leapt up onto the RCA boardroom table at one point to enthusiastically point out how good the name would look on a hoarding. RCA still wasn't convinced.

The result of the German sessions was an avant-garde album, 1981's *In The Garden*, a record with a strong bass sound, an often swirling guitar feel, and dislocated, ambient samples. It is much calmer than the frenetic noise of The Tourists, with far better production, at times sounding like The Cure around the time of 'Close To You'. With abstract lyrics on tracks like 'Belinda', it was an appealingly melancholic mixture of sounds.

"We've tried to take some of the energy that came out of the punk movement, the sweetness of soul music and the alienation of European, synthetic, mechanical rhythm and blend it together into Eurythmics music," announced the group.

The struggle begins

A taster was the first ever Eurythmics single, released from the album in mid-1981, 'Never Gonna Cry Again'. It was promoted with a performance on British television's alternative music programme, *The Old Grey Whistle Test*, featuring Clem Burke on drums,

Challenging the visual perception of women in pop, an Annie trademark from early on.

> **"We've tried to take some of the energy that came out of the punk movement, the sweetness of soul music and the alienation of European, synthetic, mechanical rhythm and blend it together into Eurythmics music."**
> *An early manifesto for Eurythmics*

Light at the end of the tunnel: Eurythmics was the vehicle to pull together the ideas shared by Dave and Annie.

Roger Pomphrey on guitar and The Slits' Penny Tobin on keyboards. The video was banned because Czukay and Liebzeit were not in the British Musician's Union. Neither that single, nor follow-up 'Belinda' did too well.

The album itself was also received with indifference from the public when it came out in the Autumn, but managed to pleasantly surprise the old guard of Tourists-hating music journalists:

"There's enough of quality to suggest that these two Tourists, at least, have finally come home," said the normally grouchy *New Musical Express (NME)*. They were able to take further encouragement from well received early gigs. They played with backing tapes at the Barracuda Club and Heaven Club in London in 1982, Annie dispelling her old punky image by wearing a black wig.

Young Diva: The focal point of Eurythmics.

Fired by the knowledge that they could at least cut it live, they decided to do another single. They thought the main problem before had been that "when we worked with other people within the record company, someone was forever coming in and saying, 'This is the guy who's doing this for you'. And it never turned out right, because the ideas all came from us, but then they'd be taken out of our hands." They went out on their own, trying to make it without Conny Plank and their management, Arnakata.

Annie and Dave were not alone in hankering after complete control: at that time Andrew Eldritch was also setting up his own Merciful Release label through WEA Records, to promote The Sisters of Mercy, a band who

> "I think it's funny—they call me an albino Grace Jones; some say I look like David Bowie 'cause of the red hair... Recently, I've been compared to Brian Eno."
> _Annie on early press perception of her image!_

Male or female? Annie's pigeonhole dodging has always been half the fun.

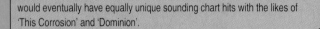

would eventually have equally unique sounding chart hits with the likes of 'This Corrosion' and 'Dominion'.

Taking control

Eurythmics set up in Chalk Farm, London with the help of one-time Selector bassist Adam Williams and his equipment. Dave augmented the studio with a bank loan: "We really had nothing going," he said of that time. "Everyone thought we were nuts. People all said 'Listen, this is unhinged. You're too far out there. You're not gonna pull anything off'—especially when we told them we were making our next album in an eight-track studio in a warehouse!

"I learned everything from maintaining a studio to how much equipment costs, to video budgets, to paying trucking

Heart shaped box of sweet dreams.

companies. We had no manager, even when 'Sweet Dreams' was at [US] Number 1. Just about everything you could imagine to do with running a group, I found out about it."

Feeling the pressure

By now they felt they had done everything they could. They lent their initials to form a company, DNA, from which to run things. Yet subsequent singles, 'The Walk' and 'This Is The House', were still poorly marketed by RCA and just didn't take off. The pressure was building up. It was tough seeing these good songs passed over, and Annie was seriously affected.

"My self-esteem dropped to an all-time low. And I was suffering from agoraphobia. I couldn't go outside the front door—whenever I went out, I started having panic attacks. I would get palpitations and come out in

The artwork and design for the band, as precise and unusual as the sound itself.

> "We really had nothing going. Everyone thought we were nuts. People all said 'Listen, this is unhinged. You're too far out there. You're not gonna pull anything off'."
> *Dave on the difficult early days*

cold sweats. It was horrible and I had a kind of breakdown." Psychotherapy proved to be no help: it was a long time before she entirely recovered, and the only positive part of the whole time was that at least her agitated emotions could be put to good use in her songwriting. And while all this trauma made for passionate songs, the public airing of her inner chaos would always be a dichotomy for such an essentially private person.

It seemed as if things could get no worse, but they

Eurythmics enjoy masked cello playing in a field antics for the 'Sweet Dreams...' video.

> "My self-esteem dropped to an all-time low. And I was suffering from agoraphobia. I couldn't go outside the front door—whenever I went out, I started having panic attacks."
> *Annie on the difficult early days*

did. During the same period, Dave had to undergo a serious lung operation in a London hospital and with that, suddenly, life had got a lot lower than before. Supporting each other, somehow the two musicians managed to survive, continue struggling and get through one of the bleakest periods of their lives.

Sweet dreams of making it

Slowly, the fortunes of the band began to improve. The first sign that things were changing came with the help of one man in RCA who still had faith. Together with the work of their graphics artist Laurence Stevens, who had provided the distinctive Eurythmics/DNA images and lettering, the band was being given a designer image and commercial push more appropriate to the Eighties. What they needed

A long way from The Tourists, a lifetime away from playing classical music.

43

> "We try to make a double-edged sound on purpose, so if you've got a really doomy lyric the song sounds at first listening like a really bubbly pop song, and if there's an up, over-the-top lyric then the music is really doomy. It's a way of infiltrating people's minds."
> *Dave revealing the secret of Eurythmic songwriting*

for complete success was a more commercially acceptable structure to their song frameworks, that still kept their musical individuality intact.

They got near to cracking it with the 'Love Is A Stranger' single in late 1981. Initially, they had problems making a video, RCA being reluctant to fund it after the 'Never Gonna Cry Again' promo was never even shown. The eventual £12,000 ($24,000) film made an impressive impact, with unusual images that

In full warpaint, promoting the newfound success with everything she's got.

didn't betray the shoestring budget it was made on in reality. Annie had moved on from the rather one-dimensional possibilities of her punk days, wearing a wig at one point and then appearing as a whore and later in bondage gear for the video. She also wanted discarded syringes scattered around in the video to make the "love as a drug" image even more explicit (this was later dropped on the grounds that the video would never be shown).

Video power

The video would also draw attention to the group in America. At that time, Music TeleVision (MTV) was

A futuristic scene from the strange, bold 'Sweet Dreams...' video. Annie would never be accused of being shy and retiring.

relatively new, and striking young English bands, including Duran Duran and Depeche Mode, were making quite an impression. Annie's own inimitable impression of a prostitute in a car whipping off a blonde wig to reveal cropped orange hair, proved a little too striking. The censors pulled the video mid-transmission, insisting there would be no more Eurythmics on TV until Annie furnished legal proof that she was a woman and not an American-youth-corrupting transvestite!

It was different on the other side of the Atlantic. In decadent Britain, they won *Music and Video Week*'s video of the year award. The single was promoted by the first tour with a real drummer rather than a backing track, but didn't do spectacularly well in the charts, partly because the video wasn't sufficiently exposed. But it didn't matter so much now. The visual and musical images of Eurythmics had combined to really get them noticed. The next release, everyone thought, should be the one to take them to the top.

The breakthrough

The original plan for a follow-up had been to release a cover of soul standard 'Wrap It Up'. This was abandoned at the last minute in favour of trying to establish themselves further with another grinding tour of original and cover material during the harsh winter of 1982. Then came the release of that album recorded on eight track. It was called *Sweet Dreams (Are Made Of This)*.

It really broke Eurythmics to the world, vindicating Laurence

Singer or Bladerunner replicant? A stark look for Eurythmics.

> "We purposely wrote songs that would free her voice, songs that she could really get into."
> *Dave on Sweet Dreams..., the album*

Stevens' starkly designed cover which RCA had taken a lot of convincing to accept. Annie used the record to explore a range of subjects, from 'This City Never Sleeps' about her time in a miserable bedsit, through 'Jennifer', based on Ophelia in a version of *Hamlet* she had seen as a child. With Dave's indispensable contribution to the sound and feel of the music, Annie was able to fully realise her vocal and lyrical potential.

"They're equipped to do it, too," said an enthusiastic music paper review. "Since here Annie Lennox at last fully exploits the most expressive realities of her … voice—something few of our current synthopop heroes and heroines would be capable of doing even if it occurred to them."

By improvising and crafting, Dave was refining his

Videos gave Annie a chance to use acting abilities for different characters.

atmosphere, which is how people used to record in the early days of rock'n'roll," declared Dave. "We purposely wrote songs that would free her voice, songs that she could really get into."

Dreams become reality

Now the band had something solid to work from, with good reviews and a good sound. When the actual 'Sweet Dreams…' single came out, it was the hit to showcase Annie's voice that everyone had been waiting for, loved by critics and public alike. The cover was equally strong, displaying Annie with her wrists tied.

One of the last songs to be written for the album, 'Sweet Dreams…' had been composed after a row between Dave and Annie. She later explained what the song was about: "I'm talking about dreamers who seek

Annie as the betrayed club singer, Dave as the two-timing hairdresser's nightmare.

production abilities so the basic eight track sound was able to compete with the best technology around. "The reason why some of our recordings sound so good and our vocal sounds are different, is because I record for

> "It's not like I know who I am all of a sudden because I'm rich. But I have carved a niche for myself. I don't have to wear a ra-ra skirt, but I can wear makeup. I can do what I want."
> *Annie Lennox on making it*

their dreams through their awareness of reality. The song is a personal statement about people's motivations, in their lives, their own dreams. And everywhere I look—'Travelled the world, and the seven seas'—all I see is that every person on the earth is looking for some kind of fulfilment. Most people don't like to look life in the face. I'm including myself. What I'm seeking is solitude through my music."

The attention of the pop public, both in Britain and America, through MTV, was also grabbed by the video. It was an inventive image, Annie and Dave in the RCA boardroom sporting matching suits, while a cow wandered in and out of shot contentedly chewing the cud. Eurythmics would become well-known for arresting videos, working together with the input of other creative people to make groundbreaking promos. While Dave hatched odd storylines, Annie produced startling image changes, haunting film/music outfitters for suitably bizarre costume concoction.

"I spent two years after the

demise of The Tourists coming to terms with this thing called image. I went through the whole stage of saying 'what am I?' The image of Annie Lennox of The Tourists was so strong and easy to pick out—I just wanted people to realise I'm not this nice, popsy,

Convincing as a man—right down to the designer stubble.

Adding that special touch to live performances.

happy-go-lucky Annie, whom I detest. So I decided to kill her, dead!" The Annie of The Tourists was a completely different creature to the new Annie of 'Sweet Dreams…'. Now she had cropped orange hair and a suit that would make her a gay and feminist idol and give the press a chance to speculate about whether Annie herself was straight, gay or something else entirely. This bold image wasn't a totally calculated one, though: "The luminous orange colour was a mistake I made with henna, which I happened to like!"

Back in a band

The successful new releases meant another tour was inevitable. With Annie on vocals and flute, Dave on guitar and keyboards, Clem Burke on drums, Mickey Gallagher of Ian Dury and the Blockheads on keyboards and backing vocalist Eddi Reader, Eurythmics played 22 dates in February and March 1983. They were by then getting a different reaction from the press, who had disliked The Tourists and had been generally indifferent to early Eurythmics. By the time the band finished their tour at London's Lyceum, the reputation had turned around and they were the press darlings—the only reservations came from the

> "I have to psyche myself up for a gig, like an athlete in training for the big race. I talk myself into fever pitch and sometimes it gets so intense that I panic onstage, even hallucinate."
> *Annie on performing in early Eurythmics*

duo themselves. They were uneasy with being back in a proper band again.

"We do feel a bit restricted at the moment in this band format," Dave admitted, "but it's the only way we could translate this album on to stage without it feeling cold." The same line-up took Eurythmics to an initially baffled Europe, where a new audience was being won over until Dave had to call the tour short after falling ill.

Everyone wanted a piece of Eurythmics once they got known. RCA was first to cash in on all the fuss, quickly re-releasing 'Love Is A Stranger' which nipped up to UK Number 6, also asking the band to do a gig

'Right By Your Side' was an unusually upbeat song for the group.

Impressive moves for
Touch's cover shoot.

for MTV to film. This was done in Heaven, a London club, with a new band behind Annie and Dave: Pete Phipps on drums, Vic Martin on keyboards, Dean Garcia on bass and backing singers The Three Croquettes. The change left the old band feeling rather abandoned but Dave and Annie felt it was important to do things on their own terms. They wanted to avoid recruiting musicians permanently for fear of another restrictive band setup like The Tourists.

"It was a very good bad experience that made us learn a lot very quickly," she explained of that old band. "And we just don't want to repeat the mistakes." Often this would result in other musicians being frozen out, but it also gave some people useful exposure. Annie's previous backing singer, Eddi Reader, became reconciled to being replaced, later using the talent she'd shown to front Fairground Attraction (best known for classic breezy-pop hit, 'Perfect').

But, as Dave was to discover, starting from scratch with a new band for the MTV show also presented difficulties: "It was the first time we'd ever played live with that line-up. We were almost forced into doing it— they said they wanted something for MTV. The band had been together for four days—some of them had never been on stage before. And Annie had laryngitis. It's the first time we've ever had anything happen that went out of our control."

> "To think of someone kissing their own ideal projection of what a man should be but to come back on themselves, to also be that man, it was great!"
> *Annie on playing with gender in video*

Empire building

Now, at least, it was possible to retreat from the commercial wolves to a truly peaceful studio. The hub of Eurythmics' operations moved to a new studio, The Church, in London's Crouch End. DNA also began to expand, including a former tour manager for Spinal Tap-like heavy metal monsters, Uriah Heep, as a PA, and Dave let the management side go to other people as it got bigger. DNA would be a parent to other video and music companies as Eurythmics' stature grew to world-wide, mind-boggling proportions.

Finally Eurythmics were big news. Another single followed later in 1982, 'Who's That Girl', accompanied by an unconventional video, with Annie as a club singer two-timed by her roguish man. Dave, naturally, was said heartbreaker, flamboyantly entering the club with shades and a succession of gorgeous women from Hazyfantazee, Bucks Fizz as well as Bananarama (whose members included Siobhan Fahey, the future Mrs D Stewart) and Marilyn, a notorious cross-dresser. Annie finally got to kiss and go off with her own handsome lover—actually Annie herself in drag. It was rapidly becoming a feature of Annie Lennox videos that her stories of love should have a quirky twist to them: "To think of someone kissing their own ideal projection of what a man should be but to come back on themselves, to also be that man, it was great!"

The obligatory promotional tour took place in mid-1983, with the typically English seaside-summer title of "Kiss Me Quick", the single topping the US charts and making Number 3 in the UK. The Eurythmics' name was now big enough for them to undertake a few

> "Happiness is a personal thing. I keep my head up, but I'm not a happy person, not generally happy... I'd rather not say what kind of person I am."
> *Annie Lennox reveals a melancholic outlook on life*

European festivals, ending with a gig played in Dalymont Park, Ireland. They played in front of a 20,000 crowd, a recognition of their achievements that was only spoilt by some unpleasant nationalistic heckling from some of the audience.

The winning touch

'Who's That Girl?' was followed by the *Touch* album in October 1983, a result of all Eurythmics' musical experimentation in their own studio. Both Annie and Dave had wanted a completely different feel to that of the first album and what they came up with was a musical balance. It was a mixture of that European feeling that "the world might end tomorrow, alongside that Afro-American exuberance and release," according to Dave.

The design work looked just as unique as the music sounded, with a cover featuring Annie masked and flexing her muscles dominatingly. Her image for the *Touch* promotional tour in the USA and the UK was enhanced by some clothes from designer Jeff Banks, Annie performing live in spite of recurring throat problems. The band also squeezed in a filmed performance for the uplifting 'Right By Your Side' single. This was an unusually upbeat, Brazilian carnival of a song showing a cheerful facet to Annie's character, albeit fleetingly: "Happiness is a personal thing," she

Lighthearted wearing of platforms and flares, unaware that years later they'd be fashionable again for real.

asserted. "I keep my head up, but I'm not a happy person, not generally happy… I'd rather not say what kind of person I am."

On the single cover, Annie, always sure of the image she wanted to portray in humorous as well as serious mood, appeared in platform soles and a glitter suit, another Jeff Banks creation.

Staying at the top

It seemed as if Eurythmics were on a roll and could do no wrong. The single and second album were winners and the new year of 1984 dawned with another classic chart-topper from *Touch*, 'Here Comes The Rain Again'. All that was needed now was to really consolidate their position. This was to be hard work, and the next few months would be anything but easy. Personally and professionally, there were many problems and pitfalls lurking in wait for Annie. It was a fairly sure bet, though, that if all the traumas the two had suffered in the past hadn't stifled their creativity so far, they wouldn't give up creating and fighting. The future looked crammed full of possibility.

'SOME OF THEM WANT TO USE YOU'

'**H**ere Comes The Rain Again' kicked off 1984 with a hit and was a classic example of how the best Eurythmics material often came out of the rows between Annie and Dave. The battles would give way to the bursts of creativity which made Eurythmics such an inspired writing partnership.

Dave's feeling was that the arguments were inevitable: "It's kind of fiery... Because we lived together. It's like writing songs with your ex-wife. But underneath it all we're much stronger, so the argument will never last more than ten minutes, whereas before it

Composed before the storm. 1984 (For The Love Of Big Brother) would cause problems.

Running around in a nightie with the rain coming again. Annie's just asking for a nasty cold.

would last three hours. We don't actually get on each other's nerves as people, but we fall out over artistic things. We're both quite headstrong and sometimes we go in different directions."

The video for the cold, haunting air of 'Here Comes The Rain…' was suitably atmospheric—hardly surprising given the location shooting in the bitterly chilly Orkneys. Annie Lennox had quickly learned the subtleties of making videos, bringing her acting abilities and eye for characters to the fore in the promos the band made, as well as showing quite a knack for understanding lighting and camera techniques. 'Here Comes The Rain…' was another of those crafted films which made Eurythmics ideally suited to the video Eighties, the two stars playing off each other well.

"Right at the beginning, I was aware that any serious personality input from me would just capsize

Eurythmics quickly became successful after years of obscurity.

the Eurythmics 'thing'," revealed Dave. "In Eurythmics it's always Annie's psyche that's kind of on display. I'll play a counterpart—like in videos—to help diffuse it sometimes or to build it up. If you notice early press shots there's Annie right up front and a bit of the back of my head somewhere."

Back on the road

The rest of the year was spent building on their reputation, which had spread fantastically quickly considering the years battling to get anyone to take notice of them at all, but first they took a break. Annie went off to sort out problems with her throat, before the band set out for an exhausting tour of more than 170 dates. The line-up this time included Dean Garcia again on bass, Olle Romo on drums, Pat Seymour on keyboards, Molly Duncan and Dave Plews on brass and The Three Croquettes backing once more. It was their fullest sound to date, exuberant despite the unwelcome return of Annie's throat troubles.

The intensive playing and frequent appearances made for a hectic lifestyle, underlining how much rock'n'roll was a fractured way of working. All the effort had brought achievement and with it came as many pressures for Annie as had obscurity. Limelight wasn't so trying for the more extrovert Dave, who positively thrived on all the trappings of pop life, while Annie found it difficult to gain stability—Eurythmics worked practically non-stop. They had both had other partners since splitting up personally, but Annie had not really found calm with anyone she wanted to be with on a long-term basis.

Krishna love

That changed at a gig in February of 1984, where a fan left vegetarian food outside Annie's hotel room, prepared in accordance with his religious beliefs. He was Radha Raman, a Hare Krishna monk, and Annie Lennox was impressed by him. Their relationship was restricted by the requirements of his faith to begin with, but she was so won over by his personality and what she saw as the spiritual quest he was on, that marriage was on the horizon within a very short time. As an enormous amount of media fuss would be inevitable, Dave gleefully provided a tabloid smoke screen by announcing a totally fake engagement to rock celebrity Nona Hendryx in full showbiz style, while Annie married Radha quietly at the same time that March.

The band toured extensively in 1984, Annie still a flautist at heart.

Travelling the world and the seven seas, arriving at gigs in a limo.

Wearied by the materialism of the pop world, struggling to establish Eurythmics and shake off Tourist debts. Lennox become enthused by some aspects of Krishna and of vegetarianism. She had been involved in some aspects of Buddhist chanting before, the Krishna element was just more publicized by her marriage. And even then it was still tempered by her primary devotion to music:

"Krishna consciousness isn't something where one has to go into a temple. disappear and become a recluse, which would have been of no interest to me because I feel that my function as a musician is a very valid one. It really started to interest me when I saw that I could integrate it with my activities." When there

> "Radha wasn't particularly attractive, but I thought I had found someone who was genuinely on a kind of spiritual quest."
> *Annie Lennox on first husband, Radha Raman*

was time between tours, Radha and Annie lived together in Switzerland, and for a while it seemed as if she had finally found stability. Her father wasn't so enamoured of her choice, and it was partly to assert her own self that she married Raman so quickly. The result was a pretty poor relationship with her father for a long while:

"It was my statement to him that 'you can't tell me what to do with my life anymore'," Annie later realized. "I had to say to him, 'I'm not your little girl. Let me make this mistake. Give me the respect to make this mistake. Give me the right', and he wouldn't. I was pretty severe with him. He wouldn't speak to me for a year. And I wouldn't speak to him."

Breaking the mould

Annie was prepared for problems in her personal life and resigned to her off-stage activities attracting public interest. But the sheer amount of prying into her privacy once she had become recognized took her by surprise. Everyone suddenly wanted to know about her husband and her social persona. The press were anxious to label her as something, whether as a bimbo pop singer or an image-changing gender-bender, while she had a

reluctance to fit any mould.

Compromise often seemed unavoidable, most notably when Eurythmics were asked to play at the 1984 Grammy Awards in America. Attending the yearly celebration of the music industry was just the sort of conformist behaviour that Annie disliked. If it wasn't what they would choose to do ideally, commercial interests pressured them into it and they decided to do it with a typical Eurythmical twist, Annie appearing as realistic Elvis lookalike, Earl the rocker. It backfired when the audience didn't immediately cotton on to the fact that this was a joke, and decided it must have been some meaningful statement.

"I didn't want to upset people—I wanted to have a little fun, that's all," Annie commented. "Americans are famous for their sense of humour. I just wanted to give them something they didn't expect. I wanted to be perplexing and mysterious. It was a joke, but I think people often see me in a serious vein. Now I know I have to spell it out when I'm trying to be light or funny."

With all the promoting and falling in love of 1984, there was no new recorded material until November. Fans had to be happy with other 'product', not always launched with Dave and Annie's full blessing. A case in

The Lennox unnerving stare, at full power in Eurythmics.

point was the May release of a full length *Sweet Dreams…* video, comprising a mix of promo and live material filmed for MTV in 1983. It wasn't the sort of challenging thing the band would have issued themselves, and they didn't sanction it. They also frowned on a dancey reworking of *Touch* tracks by mixers Jellybean and Kevorkin released by RCA under the predictably inspiration-free title of *Touchdance*.

"They made it, not us," said Annie. "I don't like it."

Some of them want to abuse you

Eurythmics were more successful in preserving artistic integrity when they moved quickly to stop RCA allowing their music to be used in adverts. Having worked so hard to establish herself as a credible, female singer, Annie was determined to avoid anything at all that smacked of selling out.

"Mary Quant cosmetics approached us, but I would never promote makeup. Too many people make too much money out of it. Vidal Sassoon offered us a load of money to advertise hair, we've been asked to advertise sunglasses, to model clothes… just loads of things. They're coming in every day—and we say no to them all. Obviously, when there's a lot of money being

Despite recurring throat problems, Annie put a lot into singing on the* Touch *tour.

offered, I'm not going to be untruthful and say that I just dismiss it like that. I dismiss it because I think it's detrimental to grab for money."

A potentially lucrative offer to do music for a sequel to the enormously popular film *Flashdance* was also turned down. On the other hand, when they were asked to do the soundtrack to a version of George Orwell's *1984*, that seemed just the great opportunity for experimentation and broadening their experience that they had been looking for. They took it despite other commitments, including Dave's work with the likes of Tom Petty.

Double plus ungood

Starring John Hurt and Richard Burton, *1984* was the hyped film of the year, and Eurythmics produced a full album's worth of music, released in November. Then it all went sour, because of a simple but crucial breakdown in communication. The original approach to do the film had been made by Virgin Films, rather than by director Michael Radford. What Dave and Annie didn't realize was that Radford already had what he thought was a perfectly serviceable soundtrack.

The Grammy Awards audience of 1984 were roundly fooled when Annie's 'Who's That Girl' alter-ego made a reappearance.

The keyboard star.

He was pressured into replacing the first score to make way for Eurythmics, leaving him with furious feelings which he revealed during a speech acknowledging an award for the film. Radford launched an outraged attack on the Eurythmics' artistic integrity for "foisting" *1984 (For The Love Of Big Brother)* on him. Dismayed Eurythmics hotly replied that they stood by the album, hadn't known there was already a score and added that they certainly wouldn't have put one forward if they had.

Lost in all this was the music itself, which did actually fit in well with the film. But the music press mistook the record for a follow-up to *Touch*, rather than a soundtrack, and condemned it for being atmospheric rather than poppy. There was one major exception to the mood-music feel of the album, the single 'Sexcrime (nineteen-eighty-four)', which reached UK Number 4 accompanied by a menacing Orwellian video.

Don't look back

The fuss faded after a while. Eurythmics still had massive popularity and *1984...* just furthered their aim of always doing something new and experimental. That they were so diverse and collaborated with other people inevitably meant that the press always liked to run rumours that they were on the verge of splitting up.

Getting involved in movies would not always be this fun.

The truth was, they still had plenty of ideas and drive.

"The only way I could describe our musical direction is to say we never stop learning, and each influence is apparent on our songwriting and recordings," affirmed Dave. "It's difficult to stake a direction for yourself without being preconceived and creating a trap for yourself."

Annie had her own theory on how it all worked: "Dave is my very good external and internal barrier. We work together lyrically and he works like an editor. I usually say a song is rubbish, and he looks at what I've done. It's strange. I'm pessimistic about my own efforts—I think they're no good. It rather takes his encouragement, helping me to see what's good in a shared vision. That way I get inspired and

> "You can't run on a broken leg. But I don't want to talk about it. It's too negative. Talking about my voice being fucked up is the worst thing I can do. It's just made me depressed."
> *Annie Lennox on recurring vocal problems*

An atmospheric video accompanied 'Sexcrime...' into the charts.

have the guts to go away and do it quietly in a corner somewhere.

"It's so important for me to stress that I'm only doing what I'm doing today because of Dave," she said

at another point. "Without him I don't think I would have stood a hope in hell. I would have been like thousands, millions of other women singers who have great potential but get nowhere."

Run away from you

Music didn't come back to the fore immediately after the problems with *1984...* Only a few months after marrying, Lennox and Raman's relationship was deteriorating. By February 1985 they had separated, not that Annie was allowed to forget the whole affair for a long while. The very idea of a female pop star having a relationship with a Hare Krishna monk got the British tabloids dribbling salaciously and they weren't about to let go of it. Even years later, an article about Annie in *The Sun* was headlined "My marriage torment to sex-mad Krishna monk" and it didn't help that a former friend and Eurythmics video producer later sold his view of the story to the *News Of The World*.

The best antidote to all this strife and the mixed reaction to *1984...* was a brisk return to the sort of work which would make an incisive response to critics—Dave and Annie got right back to basics, back to rocky roots. Their sound had gone from the synthesizer of

After the Touch tour Annie would take a break from live extravaganzas.

Left: 1985's Be Yourself Tonight *came after problems with the 1984 soundtrack and Annie's relationship with Radha Raman.*

'Sweet Dreams...' to the atmosphere of *1984...*, and now a more raucous record appeared in *Be Yourself Tonight,* released in April 1985. It once more showcased Annie's talent for writing lyrics that were emotional, yet that still had a quality that was both alienating and metaphysical, with lines like "Could this be reactivating/All my senses dislocating?" on 'There Must Be An Angel (Playing With My Heart)'. It also gave Dave a chance to let rip and show off his ridiculously fuzzed blues-widdling, on tracks like 'I Love You Like A Ball And Chain'.

Caught by the throat

A decision was made not to tour the album to save Annie further problems with her throat. Annie said: "You can't run on a broken leg. But I don't want to talk about it. It's too negative. Talking about my voice being fucked up is the worst thing I can do. It's just made me depressed." The same condition meant that they didn't appear at the British end of Live Aid, the gigantic event

Right: Stevie Wonder played dazzling harmonica on 'There Must Be An Angel...'.

by a few special guests collaborating on the album itself. One of the most special of all for Annie Lennox was long-time idol, Stevie Wonder, who contributed a harmonica solo on the track 'There Must Be An Angel (Playing With My Heart)'. Wonder had been one of her big influences as a child when she was first discovering pop and soul back in Aberdeen.

"Stevie Wonder seemed to have a new definition of perfection, instead of the precision with the flute that the school had drilled into me. Those songs touched me—the joy, the freedom, the form of expression." The feeling hadn't changed years later. "To hear Stevie Wonder playing on a song that was dedicated to him anyway was heaven." A celestial feeling which was

staged that summer to raise money for famine relief, although Annie had been one of the singers on the vinyl version of the fund raiser, supergroup Band Aid's 'Do They Know Its Christmas?'.

The lack of live appearances was compensated for

> **"Stevie Wonder seemed to have a new definition of perfection... To hear him playing on a song that was dedicated to him anyway was heaven."**
> *Annie on meeting a childhood idol*

Shy, retiring Dave Stewart in the video for 'There Must Be An Angel...'.

carried into the video, where a divine Annie in white sings for Dave, opulently made-up as a monarch, and clearly relishing every second of his hammy role.

In the court of the Sun King

Comfortable with making videos now, the film was Annie's conception, replete with floating cherubs and a full choir. It was a shamelessly over-the-top effort that suited the song completely. The band was back on commercial form, with the single hitting UK Number 1

Seeing clearly now. At the Montreux Rock Festival.

and staying in the charts for 13 weeks. Years later, cult techno group Utah Saints would sample the lyrics to great effect for a hit with 'What Can You Do For Me'.

Eurythmics were now a really unstoppable, world-dominating band, a triumph that helped Annie put her marriage firmly behind her. Still mainly vegetarian when they played the Montreux Pop Festival that year, she had nevertheless moved away from Raman's influence enough to appear in characteristic leathers. *Be Yourself Tonight* repaid the newfound confidence with two more hit singles.

The first was a duet with another soul legend, this time Aretha Franklin. It was an acclamation of women's spirit, which showcased some splendid vocal

> **"I think Eurythmics are a commercial group, but at the same time I don't think we've ever had to do anything that was really a sellout because we have always insisted that we know best what we're doing."**
> *Annie Lennox*

pyrotechnics from the two soul singers, on 'Sisters Are Doin' It For Themselves'.

Singing with a legend

The song was to make the UK Top 10 in autumn 1985, despite a shaky start to the partnership of Lennox and Franklin, who had found it initially difficult to get on with each other. Aside from personal differences, Aretha also reckoned that the line "The inferior sex are still superior" was a little too strong (in the end it was sung

Aretha Franklin's classic voice was used to full rooftop-raising effect on 'Sisters Are Doin' It For Themselves'.

> **"I think women are great, and I think men are great, and people are wonderful, potentially, when they're not killing each other."**
> *Annie Lennox on the emotion behind 'Sisters Are Doin' It For Themselves'*

"The inferior sex have got a new exterior"). The lyrics seemed to represent a departure from previous sources of inspiration for Annie. She had never really shown a political side to herself before, despite her striking character and image making her a beacon for gay and feminist activists. The single's packaging contributed to this feel, issued in different covers portraying women at work. But both Annie and Aretha found agreement in actually not wanting the song to be taken as radical.

"We aren't gonna take anything over because a man still loves a woman and a woman still loves a man," Annie said succinctly. "'Sisters…', you see, is simply a song about women. I think women are great, and I think men are great, and people are wonderful, potentially, when they're not killing each other. I don't have to say 'I bleed!' or 'I won't have anything to do with men'. Some of my best friends are men! … I don't

want to be the head of a movement. I'm singing purely out of my satisfaction, my good feeling about women. And men as well, for allowing women to do that."

High times and low times

The impressive roll-call of hits was rounded off at the end of the year with 'It's Alright (Baby's Coming Back)' reaching UK Number 12, the video depicting Annie astrally projecting to meet her lover's spirit. It was a high point to end 12 months that had seen dark moments to match all the successful times. The worst was the illness of Annie's father which would end in his death from cancer, something that made Annie Lennox herself piercingly aware of her own mortality.

"Sometimes I'm surprised I'm walking around in this bag of bones and I haven't had every limb smashed, I've been in so many near-misses," would be her opening comment in an interview after her father's death. "And when my father died this year and I saw cancer and what it does to people, I thought about my own fragility and the fragility of the human race and how we can so easily take it all for granted. As we do."

It had been a full few months packed with experience, and in 1986 she would begin to move away from the position she had taken on 'Sisters', and find a determination to become involved in big issues. Annie had already become well known for being

Sisters together. Tina Turner was originally approached to sing 'Sisters...'.

A jaunty Annie caught with Elvis Costello in relaxed, yet elegant, rockstars reclining on a sofa mode. Elvis provided harmony vocals on 'Adrian' from Be Yourself Tonight.

> "It's not an intellectual choice, it's an emotional thing. I choose what I feel. It's heartfelt and very committed. It has to be, because it represents me. If it doesn't represent me, it's not any good. That's all."
>
> *Annie on singing soul*

individual and unique and had found more substance within herself. Now she was a long way from press comparisons of her early choice of image to the likes of David Bowie and Grace Jones.

Her strong stance, personally and professionally, was invaluable in making the rough road for women in rock a little easier—late Eighties singers like Sinead O'Connor and Michelle Shocked were to take a similarly determined line in the way they presented themselves. More recently still, the 'Riot Grrrl' wave of outspoken female stars, including Hole's Courtney Love, have been building on the foundation of respect that Lennox helped to win for women in music. And as the Eighties progressed, the world would start seeing a different and more overtly campaigning side of Annie herself.

Be yourself tonight.

79

'TRAVELLED THE WORLD AND THE SEVEN SEAS'

Reaching the pinnacle of pop was not the only goal in Annie Lennox's life. She had never been one to sit back and relax once she got to the top—she wasn't even that keen on being called a star. "To be a good musician, that was my primary concern. I had no real desire to be rich and famous and I hated being the centre of attention, which is hard to believe when you see me on stage, but nevertheless, it's true… I'm coming to terms with it, because in actuality, I am a star now. But there's an awful lot of people who start from that premise, that's their ambition."

Left: Stage performances were rare in 1985, the band even missing Live Aid because of Annie's throat troubles.

Right: Friend Chrissie Hynde with Annie. The two duetted at the 1986 Royal Albert Hall benefit for Colombian volcano disaster victims

Live Aid pointed a way to develop a different, more aware sensibility. Eurythmics hadn't been able to play at the gig, and previously Annie had not thought pop could change the world much: "I'm just not somebody for movements. I'm more of a sort of separate person." Now that feeling was altering.

Another side to Annie

She put the change of opinion to use in February 1986 while Dave was again involved in production work. Annie performed at London's Royal Albert Hall with the likes of Chrissie Hynde of The Pretenders, a friend who influenced Annie's political thinking. It was a benefit that raised £20,000 ($25,000) for the victims of a recent Colombian volcano disaster, the gig coming at a time when Annie was herself feeling particularly low after her personal tragedies: "I don't believe in anything," she was quoted as saying that year. "At this point, I don't have any faith. But that doesn't mean I'm a cynic. I just don't want to put my thinking into a belief system."

The benefit didn't mean Eurythmics had given up making waves. Back in the studio, Annie and Dave put together a new album, *Revenge*, recorded in France

Annie and Dave were a close couple, musically—still going strong when Revenge came out.

> "I'm getting very ambitious to get my voice strong so that next year, when we do concerts, it's going to be a powerhouse. I just want to make music and sing and entertain people... and be a good person."
> *Annie Lennox on preparing live* Revenge

with, unusually for the duo, a full band behind them. Annie was on the cover with eyes drawn in unnervingly similar style to those of a reptile on the inside, and there was much material on the record that put the cat among the critical pigeons. Many reviews accused it of being composed to "rock out" with, stadium-style—the most reprehensible crime a band known for being experimental could commit in the eyes of the trendy music press. It was also the first Eurythmics release to feature a cover picture of Dave and Annie equally. The picture underlined that, while Dave might be a chaotic character when compared against Annie's vocal

The band were in rock monster mode when they toured Revenge. *Audiences loved it.*

The red bra which Annie removed at a Revenge gig, confusing critics who thought only Madonna got up to that sort of thing.

precision—often seen only as the shadowy beard in the background—they were still very much a team.

"I definitely couldn't form Eurythmics with another girl," Dave had asserted, "and I don't think, if Annie went, that some other bloke could try to do what we do. It's a mixture of our personalities… It's weird how the two of us fit. We're on a similar wavelength."

Revenge of the red bra

The album was released in the summer, preceded by the single 'When Tomorrow Comes', and promoted by an ambitious, eight-month world tour, now Annie had rested her voice for a while: "I'm getting very ambitious to get my voice strong," she had told a journalist previously, "so that next year, when we do concerts, it's going to be a powerhouse. I've got that ambition now. I just want to make music and sing and entertain people… and be a good person."

More of Annie's ghosts were laid to rest by another single, 'Thorn In My Side'. With a video including Krishna-ritual elements and the main refrain "Thorn in my side/That's all you ever were", it was reputedly a dig at her former husband, Radha Raman.

Getting what they deserve

By the time the sell-out tour reached London in December, the dates at Wembley Arena were widely tipped to be the gigs of the year. The reviewers may not have gone for the anthemic appeal of 'Missionary Man' and the like on vinyl, but the public weren't put off. Live, black and white stage sets with backdrops and effects based around the pseudo-religious theme lived up to the hype. These exciting shows did their bit to send the single up the charts to UK Number 31 when it was released in early 1987.

Even the press were won over by the band live: "In

Her angular shape made Annie instantly recognizable, always electrifying in action.

1986, it is Eurythmics who call the shots, and they showed at Wembley how even their early light, archetypal synthpop hits could be invested with all the muscular bravado that they now routinely apply to their music," said one reviewer, adding: "As Annie Lennox stormed about the stage and cracked down hard on the soul revue stomp of 'Would I Lie To You?' and the bad girl grind of 'Missionary Man', it seemed not so much a sell-out, more a convincing reversion to type."

With a raw, rock feel to the live music, Annie's costume changes obligingly included her stripping down to a skimpy red bra—which was flung off at one point! That caused much anguish in the media, who didn't see the irony in the gesture and thought of Annie as better known for her dislike of women exploiting themselves in music. Even years later, a tabloid story alleged that she had refused to appear on an Australian talk show with celebrity prostitute Lindi St. Clair, and she has also commented unfavourably on

Lyrical inspiration often came from Annie's experiences in relationships; one was with dancer Billy Poveda.

pop's bimbos, like the raunchy live act of Prince's Sheila E and, of course, the very explicit scenes in Madonna videos.

" 'True Blue'... I wanted to see what all the fuss was about. Um... I can see why. I can see very clearly why. But I've listened to it once, and that sort of says it all." Annie's image, in contrast, was based around that particularly angular figure, disturbing in masculine clothes or fiercely feminine as she showed on the *Revenge* tour.

Clocking up the hits

As if countering the sweaty rock of *Revenge*, the Eurythmics' Christmas release which reached UK Number 23 was a powerful ballad, 'Miracle Of Love'. The band fiercely denied that leaving experimental synthesizer music to do rock and ballads were an indication that they had lost their creative spark:

"Run out of ideas!? Run out of ideas!! Christ, we've only just started!" was Annie's extremely irate response. "Run out of ideas! Listen... We could continue like this... FOREVER! We could do three albums a year if we wanted to. We made that album in a few weeks. It's not difficult."

A reflective Annie—'The Miracle Of Love'
would reveal a mellower side to Eurythmics.

Any unexpected direction change was bound to provoke speculation in the press, but what made matters worse was that this kind of criticism coincided with personal attacks against Lennox by vitriolic columnist Julie Birchill and *Daily Mirror* writer Lesley-Ann Jones, all of which took its toll. Annie began to retreat more and more from the press.

"It's painful," she had once said of character assassination, "but then you have to learn to see that other people's motivation is sometimes very bitter and twisted. So now I realize, yes, people will sometimes hate me. It's a paranoia that makes you try and explain everything so very carefully. God, did I go through that!" In fact, Jones' attack seemed more to be out of fear of Annie's strong persona and success than anything else. She said, after the *Revenge* tour hit London's Wembley Arena: "Clearly I am in the minority when I say I didn't like Annie Lennox. Frankly—I felt threatened by her."

Part of the gradual exit from the limelight was also due to Annie's relationship with Israeli film-maker, Uri Fruchtman. She had been linked with other men after her split from Raman, but Uri was the one who would

Annie was still exploring personal emotions in Savage, while Dave had settled down more, with a wife, Siobhan Fahey from Bananarama.

*Looking towards a **Brand New Day**, although the film of that name never got an official release.*

become her husband in 1988. The two had met during the lengthy *Revenge* tour, when Fruchtman shot a rockumentary of Eurythmics in Japan, called *Brand New Day*, after a track from the album. This film never made commercial release, slated by the press on its preview at the Edinburgh Film Festival as making Dave and Annie just look like "typical rock stars", an opinion the band themselves eventually agreed with: "It was an attempt to see the aspects of a country that we were touring, to break out of the bubble of touring. I'm very glad we made the film now, but I couldn't find my place at all. I felt out of place," said Annie afterwards.

Hormonally his

Dave was also married, in 1987, ironically to the woman who had played one of his floozies in the 'Who's That Girl?' video, Siobhan Fahey of Bananarama (and later of cult pop duo Shakespear's Sister). Stewart was anxious not to get as close to her work as he had with Annie:

"I have learned by my mistakes. I might give Siobhan's band advice, and we occasionally write songs together. But I'd never ever write songs for Shakespear's Sister. We'd turn into that same inseparable, claustrophobic mess as Annie and I were." With the media still eager to paint the women as

Annie finally found romantic happiness with second husband Uri Fruchtman.

deadly rivals in pop for Stewart's affections, Annie explained her position.

"Before he met Siobhan there were different involvements with people and he was less settled, everything felt up in the air in a sense. Now there's a structure round him, something very positive that will deepen his experience as a human being. It will also be something apart from Eurythmics… Something wonderful, enriching." The wedding was just as showbizzy and paparazzi-studded as the later marriage of Fruchtman and the glitz-shy Lennox wasn't—her marriage was to be a deeper, more stable affair than her relationship with Raman had been. It would accentuate the value of other things in life for Annie, and prompt her to move one step further away from the fast lane.

Take a girl like that

It was this kind of more reflective and introspective mood that appeared on *Savage*, which arrived towards the end of 1987. In contrast to *Revenge*, here was an unflinchingly personal work with Annie's painful emotions running through it in concept album fashion. It was, from the start, a classic Eurythmics project, the two recording in a quiet French studio without a band. Annie was more relaxed, clearer than ever about what she wanted to say, and Dave freely acknowledged the

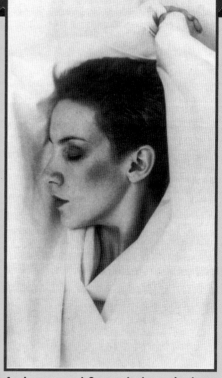

Annie composed. **Savage** *had exorcised a lot of ghosts for her, although it wasn't as commercially successful as* **Revenge***.*

Eurythmics were part of the sizeable concert staged in London, 1988, in support of ANC leader Nelson Mandela.

result was largely Annie's own statement.

"*Savage* was an annihilation record!" he told now defunct British magazine *Record Mirror* in 1989. "A lot of Annie's words were about the despair and pain of being on the receiving end of men being so horrible.

That was Annie's time out, it was almost a solo album except that I made the music with her."

They preserved a sparse quality on many of the tracks, which was a throwback to the days of *In The Garden* and *Sweet Dreams...*, the synth sound very dominant, much more than had been the case on *Be Yourself Tonight*. The personal nature of the tracks was underlined in that many of the lyrics were more acted and spitefully-spoken, than sung. Different Annie characters came to the fore in the most powerful Eurythmics way yet, before the album moved to a more acoustic feel at its conclusion.

Savage power

Savage's songs were given an added potency in their videos—all along, Eurythmics promos had a reputation for being innovative and quirky. They took this one step further with a 1988 video album of *Savage*, directed by the talented Sophie Muller and showcasing Annie's characters. There was the bored housewife who freaks out, in the single 'Beethoven (I Love To Listen To)', released October 1987, and the vamp in 'I Need A Man' of March 1987, similar to the whorish figure of 'Love Is A Stranger'. These figures reappeared in different guises all the way through, creating a linking thread which made the film much more than just promos slung together. And in ironically jaunty mode, she appeared in a mock Swiss setting to accompany 'Do You Want To Break Up?' (perhaps another jibe at former husband Radha Raman—the two had lived together in Switzerland).

"It is a kind of catharsis for me to write about pain," she explained. "But it's not just my experience. It's a whole load, these plays that had to be re-enacted. I could choose a lover who was masochistic and I was sadistic and somehow or other it had to be that person. I had to be the one for them and they had to be the one for me... That's what fascinates me." Annie used the album to explore a whole range of emotions, with the feelings left from the failed relationship with dancer Billy Poveda (who was still on good professional terms with Annie) providing some of the inspiration:

"When I wrote the songs for our new album *Savage*, I had just broken up with the man I had been living with for two years and it left me reeling," reported Britain's *Daily Express*. "I wasn't prepared for it and I felt very betrayed. It was as if my world was caving in around me."

Placing a chill in the charts

Critics were happy with what was seen as Eurythmics getting back on form, but this time it was the public who didn't flock to buy these tales of dark emotions, as they had done with the upbeat rock of *Revenge*. Only 'You Have Placed A Chill In My Heart', released in May 1988, broke the UK Top 20, with a video featuring Annie desperately hugging a man towards the end, perhaps an indication of how much the relationship with Uri Fruchtman now meant to her.

With no major tour announced, the videos had to be suffcient to promote the album, although they weren't Annie's only screen appearance at that time. She also featured in a version of Harold Pinter's *The*

Room, alongside Donald Pleasance and Julian Sands. Annie and the playwright share a common ground, in that Pinter writes to highlight the problems of communicating with other human beings, while Annie enjoys the challenge of communicating intelligently through the hackneyed vocabulary of pop.

"I think words have endless potential. Within the pop context I try to make something that's emotive and ironic. It's a challenge to redefine words that are continually being used until they're parodies of themselves. The challenge is also to find whether you yourself have still got something relevant to say, and then say it beautifully, with real depth."

Hurricane Stewart

Dave was also branching out, not into plays, but into families. Siobhan gave birth to Samuel Joseph Hurricane in November 1987, and it was only a few months later that Annie married Uri and announced

that she, too, was pregnant. Her pop career would now begin to take a definite second place to family and other aspects of her life.

Annie Lennox the singer didn't disappear altogether. Just as Dave was working with famous names on various projects, she too would do the odd collaboration—including a duet with Al Green for the Bill Murray *Christmas Carol* film, *Scrooged*. The B-Side for that featured a group called The Celestial Spheres of Influence, which was actually her and Dave again, the name they once dropped in favour of The Tourists.

Eurythmics for Mandela

Her political interests had not vanished either, sometimes overlapping into pop, as when Eurythmics played for 70,000 at the concert for ANC leader Nelson Mandela at Wembley in the summer of 1988. Without a major *Savage* tour for practice, the slot was rehearsed with a storming warmup set in London's Town and Country Club (now The Forum):

"The hour-long set was a celebration of past Eurythmics achievements as Annie whirled and Dave Stewart twirled," said the London *Evening Standard* of

> "The challenge is also to find whether you yourself have still got something relevant to say, and then say it beautifully, with depth."
>
> *Annie Lennox on the skill of writing*

Live performances would be rare for Savage, *a far cry from the lengthy* Revenge *tour.*

the T&C gig. "If there was a lack of subtlety, it was amply compensated by the sheer energy of the set."

Diversity, success, a good marriage, it seemed as if Lennox had finally achieved everything. That all shattered at the end of the year when she went into hospital to have her baby. For no particular reason, as sometimes tragically happens, the child was stillborn. She would survive the experience—the drive that had sustained Annie through all the rocky years before would not desert her now. The news spread quickly and with his own family now, Dave was also reported to have been extremely shocked.

Annie and Uri were able to see and take pictures of the baby, Daniel, which Annie felt went some way to help with the healing experience, and she bravely went on to talk publicly about what happened in an attempt to help other families who have suffered a stillbirth. Once more finding herself right in the centre of unwelcome media attention, she was fortunately shielded from most of the inquisitive tabloid newspaper reporters by her friends and management. Just at the moment she had hoped to concentrate on building and spending time with her family, the tragedy spurred her to fling herself back into work to avoid sinking into depression. Rather than dwelling on the past, Annie just forged ahead, with—not for the first time—an uncertain future ahead of her.

WE TOO ARE ONE AGAIN

I n early 1989, the British Phonographic Institute (BPI) award for Best Female Singer went to Annie, poignantly soon after the December stillbirth. All too easily she could have slipped into a black hole, as so many people faced with such a tragedy do.

Instead, the political side of her character was thrown into even greater relief, building on her work at the Mandela gig of the previous year. She added her influence to a group of high-profile musicians working on an album, released in the spring of 1989 for pressure group Greenpeace. In April, Annie travelled to Russia with other stars, including U2's The Edge and Peter Gabriel, to promote the album and the Moscow opening of a Greenpeace office. Annie was without the other half of Eurythmics on the trip, Dave having gone to Russia the year before on his own, to work with Boris Grebenshikov (Russia's leading, if not only, rock star).

Green Annie

Pleasantly surprised journalists reporting back on Annie said she seemed extremely well informed on the

Annie felt she had been snubbed by the Brits for 'artists' like ex-topless model Samanatha Fox. But when awards began finally going to Annie, they never stopped.

issues involved—anyone hoping to expose a mere Eurythmics' publicity drive was disappointed.

"Somewhere in the back of my mind for years I had the feeling that things were not quite right," she explained of her new role on the world stage. "I never

We Too Are One *was promoted by the 65 date Revival world Tour.*

voted; I was completely cynical and disillusioned with all political parties, having a sincere mistrust of all politicians. Finally, after all these years it turns out that groups like Greenpeace have been quietly working away without much exposure, and now it's just clicked, everything's gone into place. Through a union of the media and people like myself, we're sounding a clarion call. The advent of the Greens is as significant as the advent of socialism at the turn of the century. No question about that." Annie had been hot on issues such as vegetarianism and recycling before, but this trip saw her questioning more deeply.

"Obviously it's useful for both Mikhail Gorbachev and Margaret Thatcher to be seen to be Green," she

The Revival Tour had a back to basics feel about it, showcasing songs rather than pyrotechnics.

realized. "But then Margaret Thatcher keeps promoting nuclear power, which in our country is one of the main ecological issues. One could be very cynical about the Russians inviting us here to put a human face on things, but what do you do, just pack up and go home?"

The last album

It was now almost two years since any new Eurythmics records. Dave had filled the time, as usual, with producing, collaborating and boozing with famous mates, while Annie's private tragedies now pushed her

> "I had this vision constantly towards the end of the Eurythmics period: my life was a bus, but I was running behind it, I just could not catch up with that fucking bus."
> *Annie Lennox*

back into the studio faster than she would have liked. The result was that a new album was fairly quickly completed, and the band played the usual chat and pop show circuit. Yet first single 'Revival' only just scooted into the UK Top 30, hitting Number 26.

End of an era

And this wasn't just another Eurythmics single. It came at the end of a decade throughout which Dave and Annie had been making music as Eurythmics. When the album, *We Too Are One*, was released with a huge promotional budget in September, it marked the end of an incredible nine years of output. It was a well received offering, making UK Number 1 and inspiring press comments like "When it comes to making songs that catch in your head and tickle the subconscious, Dave and Annie are still awfully accomplished." But it

Right: Annie's two year break from music was partly to work with groups like Shelter and partly to try again for a family with husband Uri Fruchtman.

was also to be the last Eurythmics album—when a new decade began, Annie would be alone.

A farewell couldn't be made quietly by a group like Eurythmics, who had never exactly shied away from doing things with style and panache. The 65-date "Revival" world tour was launched in true form, with a couple of planes full of journalists flown out to Juan les Pins near Cannes, France, for a show and also an acoustic set during the press conference. It wasn't to everyone's taste.

Sun, sea and hype

Some found the media blitz a bit overwhelming, among them British music weekly *Melody Maker*. When it came to the acoustic set, they decided that "Why artists of their calibre should be doing this, putting their all into bits of their songs while a selection of hacks from all over the world chortle and gape … is a mystery beyond all fathoming.

"But when Annie lightly touches Dave's arm to signal the end of 'When The Day Comes Down' there's an instant of genuinely silent awe in the room before the rude eruption of gratuitous applause. In the midst of the circus they'd located their own private moment and, just for a second, they were more to be pitied than blamed."

Much of the organization for this first tour in two years was undertaken by Annie herself, the lineup including Chucho Merchan on bass, Olle Romo on drums again, Joniece Jameson and The Gap Band's Charlie Wilson on ebullient backing vocals and Pat Seymour on keyboards. Further singles from the album didn't fare too well in spite of this well planned tour, partly because they were suffering from the popularity of the Acid House dance craze of the late Eighties.

A new way out

'Don't Ask Me Why', a single which Dave Stewart revealed in a 1993 interview was the last song Eurythmics ever recorded together, and 'Angel' didn't do incredibly well in Britain, but made a better showing in America. If breaking America seemed an artistically compromising thing for Eurythmics to do, 'The King And Queen Of America' countered that, with Annie and Dave using the video to satirize various hackneyed portrayals of couples in the "American Dream".

The tour itself was a more stripped-down affair than had been the case with previous outings. Reviewers commented of the September London Wembley Arena dates that, "It began to seem as if there were a

> "I had no real desire to be rich and famous and I hated being the centre, which is hard to believe when you see me on stage, but nevertheless, it's true."
> *Annie Lennox on late second thoughts about her career*

deliberate back-to-basics point being made … The duo's ability consistently to write songs which shine in any number of settings was evidenced when the band went off, leaving Lennox accompanied by Stewart on 12-string acoustic guitar."

Live, Eurythmics were more relaxed, but Annie hadn't totally put her troubles behind her. The song 'Angel', which tickled UK Number 23, with its spiritualist overtones, was initially written about her aunt and then for the memory of her stillborn son. Annie was trying to deal with all her experiences as positively as she knew how and always pushed her songwriting forward—despite titles like 'You Hurt Me (And I Hate You)', the band had not meant the album to come over as being a bitter one.

"Lyrically it's important to test new limits to what

you can say. There are millions of love songs—it's time to put an extreme one about hate in there. It seems to run parallel to love in so many respects—so many love affairs have fallen foul, ended up in horrendous circumstances, I'm sure everyone knows through personal experience what I'm talking about." Eurythmics' continuing appeal was sealed with another award for Best Female Singer in the BPI ceremony of early 1990. But Annie and the man she had once shared "a very unique bond" with had decided not to collaborate again.

"I can't imagine Dave not being in my life somehow or another," she had once said. "And I think he feels the same way about me." Now they were apart. It was an amicable parting, and Dave for one had always seen the positive side of the relationship with Annie, once declaring:

"We *are* the only couple I know that lived together

> "We had an overdose of each other, didn't we? Living together, then splitting up but staying together as Eurythmics. Oh dear!"
> *Annie on life without Dave*

and then virtually in the week we stop living together, form Eurythmics and become famous as a couple. Usually it is the other way around. They get famous and then start bitching."

The split was revealed when Annie, on receiving the award at the characteristically disorganized BPI ceremony, said she was leaving music for two years. Naturally, the statement was reported with suitable shock-horror headlines in the press the next day, but it wasn't a spur of the moment idea—Annie had thought this out. Firstly, she said, she wanted to try for another baby, and it was only a few months later that she happily reported that she was once more pregnant. She also wanted to work for Shelter, an organization set up to help homeless people.

Eurythmic alone

There had already been a Eurythmic track from *We Too Are One* about the homeless, 'When The Day Goes Down'. Coupled with an adoring article in Sunday paper *The Observer*—sycophantically headlined "Pop's Queen Goes Down Among The Homeless"—it all added up to the misleading impression that she was another star just doing her high-profile bit for increased record sales. Annie had actually been in long talks with

Diva in a suit.

The Queen of Pop pays tribute to the Queen of Rock at the 1992 Freddie Mercury Tribute gig.

Shelter, and had wanted to work with them behind the scenes, using her influence to encourage contributions. She would also donate stage gear to an auction, and worked for their 25th anniversary celebration in

December 1991. Moving more and more in the direction of helping others had something to do with the manner in which she had been brought up, and her life-long love of soul.

"I suppose it's all to do with people who have some knowledge of poverty—the struggle, you know, the struggle," she had told a *Rolling Stone* journalist. "I can't say I really know the black experience, but there's something in knowing about the rich and poor and the differences in class and not being able to get this and that."

Another contribution to a campaign came with World AIDS Day in 1990. Along with many other top stars, Annie did a version of a Cole Porter song, hers being 'Every Time We Say Goodbye'. The seriousness of the issue was highlighted when her video director, Derek Jarman, had to be replaced after falling ill with an AIDS-related illness. At the same time, Dave was also involved in important issues, contributing to the *One World, One Voice* spectacular in 1990, one of many musicians to perform in a worldwide link-up.

Daughter of a showgirl

Towards the end of the year, Annie gave up work to help ensure the safe birth of her baby, who arrived on December 16, 1990, called Lola. Annie began the new year looking after her—happily—entirely healthy baby,

> "We're the only couple I know that lived together and then virtually in the week we stop living together, form Eurythmics and become famous as a couple. Usually it is the other way around. They get famous and then start bitching"
> *Dave on the odd partnership with Annie*

any solo project placed firmly on the back burner.

Shortly after Lola's birth came the first round-up of Eurythmics' career, when the *Greatest Hits* album was issued in early 1991. Their first major single, 'Love Is A Stranger' was re-released to promote it, reaching Number 46 in the UK charts. The hits package reinforced the notion that Eurythmics were unlikely to produce anything new, and the two continued to move

Gary Oldman and Winona Ryder rest Gothic accents for a nocturnal spot of kissing in the 1993 film of Dracula—the soundtrack included Annie's 'Love Song For A Vampire'.

in increasingly separate professional directions. By 1991, Dave had produced two solo albums, as well as continuing with the diversity of production and writing projects he first became involved with years before in DNA's London Church studio.

Babies and other diversions aside, Annie was also working on her own solo project, but without the more experienced Dave as a partner in music and in press interviews, she was reluctant to give much away.

"I don't know about working separately," she confessed before the Eurythmics split. "I've never done anything on my own. I'm willing to have a bash to see where my weaknesses lie and where I can turn weaknesses into strength. I don't know what I'd do without Eurythmics though." She was about to see what she could do without the group, when she overcame self-doubts to continue work on the project she'd started before she had Lola. Completed with the help of musical friends and some special guests, like

Despite fears of failure, Annie successfully reinvented herself as a solo artist in 1992.

The Blue Nile (who collaborated on a track entitled 'The Gift'), her first solo album was finally released in early 1992—*Diva*.

A happy diva

It came at a more stable time for Annie, now with the family she'd always wanted: "Everyone knowing about Daniel being stillborn and talking about it was not the best medication in the world," she said after Lola's birth. "But now I have Lola. She has changed my life in all the corny ways that children are supposed to. I have always suffered from extremes of emotion: deep depressions and mad highs. It was good for creative purposes, but it was hell for having a happy life. I'm calmer these days and it's a great relief."

Diva wasn't the radical departure from Eurythmics-style music that Annie might have taken. All the same, the album was undeniably a more mature, warmer work than the anguished outpourings Annie had frequently showcased in Eurythmic records. She felt secure enough about the songs she had written on her own to include a humorous cover version—the authentic thirties-sounding 'Keep Young And Beautiful', another ironic reference to the idea of the Diva trying to keep her looks at any cost.

Within a pop-friendly structure, Annie also used *Diva* to experiment and explore different emotions. A

> "I wanted a visual image that represented me, yet which had nothing to do with Eurythmics and I think this suits me very well. After all I am alone now and that is the essence of the Diva."
> **Annie Lennox**

dreamy, Eastern feel was used to great effect on 'Primitive'; and she recalled her early struggles in London with the strong soul of 'Legend In My Living-Room'. It explored the situation of a hopeful 17-year-old who comes to the capital city, but unlike Annie Lennox, doesn't make it big. The album was classic Lennox, from the catchy tunes to the personal lyrics—but it wasn't any easier to produce than the old Eurythmics' material.

"I knew that I wanted to prepare for this album in a very solitary way, working closely with a producer and possibly writing with other people, but definitely not using a band," she said of the process of writing. "I also knew that I wanted to take my time, releasing it only when I felt it was strong enough and not a moment before.

"I suppose the whole idea of it is that you dig deep

inside yourself for inspiration and of course, it's so much easier to do that when you're feeling completely miserable—there's all that extra grist for the mill. But I'm just not that miserable these days, so how dare I think I could write good songs!"

Back at the top

The question of whether this new direction would be accepted by others was quickly resolved. Annie admitted she would be "crushed" if the album didn't take off, but she need not have worried. She was firmly established as a completely credible solo artist by singles from the album like 'Why', which hit UK Number 5 and 'Walking On Broken Glass', which hit UK Number 8. The airy, yet still lyrically-barbed tracks were particulary refreshing in Britain, coming in the middle of an extremely dreary election campaign. Not everyone was entirely pleased, and even though she won the 1992 Ivor Novello award for 'Why' (music and lyrics), *Melody Maker*'s David Bennun was one of those who was apparently annoyed that Annie was now happy.

"Next time spare us the obligatory 'I've-Had-A-Baby-Y'Know' number," he growled, "and the Twenties musical pastiche … Stick that idea in your gripe and choke it. Help bring the snarl back to my face."

Despite that kind of response, music was important

for Annie, but still came in second place to familial responsibilities, which meant there was no enormous world tour to promote *Diva*. Her first major post-Eurythmics live appearance would be in her *Blade Runner*-type eye makeup at the large memorial Freddie Mercury gig in April 1992 which raised over £3 million ($4.5m) for AIDS research.

No tour followed after that, as the Fruchtman-Lennox family prepared to expand again. And while pregnant again in early 1993, a video for the single 'Little Bird' was made, which showed Annie hadn't lost her sense of fun in going solo. It featured actors, male and female, as Annies past and present, but wasn't her first light-hearted solo video. She had also used British comedian Hugh Laurie as a main guest in the video for 'Walking On Broken Glass', playing a Regency dandy toying with her affections in the grand setting of a sumptuous ball.

Love like blood

The new status as world-class solo singer was consolidated by winning her fifth award, the 1993 BPI Brits award for Best Album and Best Female Singer, which she seemed now to practically own. The accolade could have been marred by a big controversy caused about the awards, when allegations were made that the voting had been

The first Annie Lennox solo single, 'Why', and album, Diva, *came a few months after the birth of her first daughter, Lola.*

'rigged' on a couple of categories, but Annie was of suffdent stature to rise above it all. She also won an award for Best Video at the 1993 American Grammy Awards.

Music awards are no indication of how a performer is perceived outside the pop world, so her new status among others in the arts was only made clear when she was made a prestigious offer to contribute music for the much hyped version of Bram Stoker's novel, *Dracula.* Unlike the problems over the Eurythmics' soundtrack for *1984*, there was no outcry over 'Love Song For A Vampire', which she performed on British chart show, *Top Of The Pops.* Utah Saints, the group who had sampled her 'There Must Be An Angel…'

> "I suppose the whole idea of it is that you dig inside yourself for inspiration and of course, it's so much easier to do that if you're miserable… But I'm just not that miserable these days, so how dare I think I could write good songs!"
> *Annie Lennox on writing* Diva

vocals, contributed some remixes of 'Little Bird' to the CD 'Love Song…' single.

When an eager audience will see the next Annie effort is debatable. She has showcased her blossoming confidence as a solo artist by adding to the sizeable amount of rock's elders who have recorded an acoustic MTV *Unplugged* session, but any possibility of Eurythmics collaboration was categorically ruled out in November 1993 by Dave Stewart. He explained to British music magazine *Vox* that the band had split up mainly as a result of the constant grind of touring and recording. He revealed that although they hadn't really wanted to say so at the time, they would never be working together again. The live album which was released in that same month, *Live 1983-1989*, was, he declared, the final summation of Eurythmics—the swansong.

This last album was the result of more than one gig, featuring songs from the different Eurythmic eras. It included such gems as a 'Sweet Dreams…' recorded the week the single was released in the early Eighties.

Keeping the audience waiting

Annie herself continued to immerse herself in her family. She gave birth to another daughter, Tali, shortly after her pregnancy had forced her to accept her awards by video at the BPI ceremony in 1993. Later the same year, she moved to a new home in London's Highgate (not too far away from where Eurythmics used to record and Dave and Bob Dylan have regularly recorded—in Crouch End!). Her record company asserted in late 1993 that she hadn't left music and was working on new material, adding unhelpfully, "But then she's always working."

With two daughters now, and aged almost 40, Annie Lennox seems unlikely to want to go through the entire treadmill of the rock world again. She had already found the pop industry trying after the birth of her first baby.

"There is something about the rock'n'roll tribe that is quite ludicrous to me. The men are like pigs in muck when they get together. When they started

> "I have no plans at the moment for another album. I am in a position where I can do a record when I want to. My diary is blank and I like that. It makes me feel like a human being, not a robot."
> *Annie Lennox on finally finding happiness*

doing the lads thing I had to go to my room. It drove me slightly mad." she has said.

Legacy of a Lennox

Distaste for life on the road aside, it is difficult to imagine the driven Annie Lennox knitting babies' booties in genteel retirement, but then she has become a lot more settled in the last few years. The tabloids have had a distinct lack of bra-flinging antics to report recently, and have had to content themselves with sneaking pictures of her in casual clothes with her family. If she was to drop out of pop, one thing is certain, the music she has produced in her long career as Tourist, Eurythmic and solo artist has guaranteed the girl who wanted to be a flautist her own unique place in the history of pop.

"Professionally and personally, I have grown up," she told Breakfast TV in early 1993. "Now I have a family and that is great because it has enriched my life. I am a better person for it. My life is in perspective.

"I have no plans at the moment for another album. I am in a position now where I can do a record when I want to. My diary is blank and I like that. It makes me feel like a human being, not a robot."

A world-dominating vision. It often seemed uncertain—but Annie eventually made it.

DISCOGRAPHY

Date [UK] ...... Title (Catalogue Number [UK]) ...... British Chart ...... Weeks ...... US Chart ...... Weeks

Annie Lennox: Album (CD Catalogue Number)

Date [UK]	Title (Catalogue Number [UK])	British Chart	Weeks	US Chart	Weeks
6 Apr 1992	Diva (RCA PD 75326)	1	70	23	72

Annie Lennox: Singles

Date [UK]	Title (Catalogue Number [UK])	British Chart	Weeks	US Chart	Weeks
Oct 1988	Put A Little Love In Your Heart (with Al Green) (A&M AM 484)	28	8	9	
Mar 1992	Why (RCA CD single PD 45320)	5	8	34	
May 1992	Precious (RCA CD single 74321100252)	23	5		
Aug 1992	Walking On Broken Glass (RCA CD single 74321107222)	8	8	14	
Oct 1992	Cold (RCA CD single 74321116902)	26	4		
Feb 1993	Little Bird (RCA CD single 7432113383-2			49	

Eurythmics: Albums (CD Catalogue Numbers)

Date [UK]	Title (Catalogue Number [UK])	British Chart	Weeks	US Chart	Weeks
16 Oct 1981	In The Garden (RCA ND 75036)				
4 Jan 1983	Sweet Dreams (Are Made Of This) (RCA ND 71471)	3	60	15	59
6 Nov 1983	Touch (RCA ND 90369)	1	48	7	37
28 May 1984	Touchdance (RCA ND 75151)	31	5	15	11
Nov 1984	1984 (For The Love Of Big Brother) (Virgin CDV 1984)	23	17		
26 Apr 1985	Be Yourself Tonight (RCA ND 74602)	3	80	9	45
29 Jun 1986	Revenge (RCA PD 71050)	3	52	12	33
9 Nov 1987	Savage (RCA/BMG 74321 13440-2)	7	33	41	19
11 Sep 1989	We Too Are One (RCA PD 74251)	1	32	34	28
Nov 1990	Box Set (RCA ND 74384)				
18 Mar 1991	Greatest Hits (RCA PD 74856)	1	40	72	23
15 Nov 1993	Live 1983-1989 (RCA 74321171452)	●	●	●	●

● Book went to press as album was charting.

Eurythmics: Singles

Date [UK]	Title (Catalogue Number [UK])	British Chart	Weeks	US Chart	Weeks
28 May 1981	Never Gonna Cry Again (RCA 68)	63	3		
16 Aug 1981	Belinda (RCA RCA 115)				
25 Mar 1982	This Is The House (RCA 199)				
25 Jun 1982	The Walk (RCA 230)				
17 Sep 1983	Love Is A Stranger (RCA DA 1)	54	5		
21 Jan 1983	Sweet Dreams (Are Made Of This) (RCA DA 2)	2	14	1	
9 Apr 1983	Love Is A Stranger (RCA DA 1) —reissue—	6	8	23	
16 Jun 1983	Who's That Girl? (RCA DA 3)	3	10	21	
23 Oct 1983	Right By Your Side (RCA DA 4)	10	11	29	
7 Jan 1984	Here Comes The Rain Again (RCA DA 5)	8	8	4	
3/11/84	Sexcrime (Nineteen Eighty-Four) (Virgin VS 728)	4	13	81	
19/1/85	Julia (Virgin VS 734)	44	4		
4 April 1985	Would I Lie To You? (RCA PB 40101)	17	8	5	
21 Jun 1985	There Must Be An Angel (Playing With My Heart) (RCA PB 40247)	1	13	22	
17 Oct 1985	Sisters Are Doin' It For Themselves (RCA PB 40339)	9	11		
27 Dec 1985	It's Alright (Baby's Coming Back) (RCA PB 403775)	12	8	78	

30 May 1986	When Tomorrow Comes (RCA DA 7)	30	6	
24 Aug 1986	Thorn In My Side (RCA DA 8)	5	11	68
7 Nov 1986	The Miracle Of Love (RCA DA 9)	23	9	
13 Feb 1987	Missionary Man (RCA DA 10)	31	4	14
9 Oct 1987	Beethoven (I Love To Listen To) (RCA DA 11)	25	6	
Dec 1987	Shame (RCA DA 14)	41	5	
28 Mar 1988	I Need A Man (RCA CD single DA 15CD)	26	6	46
31 May 1988	You Have Placed A Chill In My Heart (RCA DA 16)	16	8	64
Nov 1988	Sexcrime (Nineteen Eighty-Four) (Virgin CD single CDT 22)			
4 Aug 1989	Revival (RCA CD single DACD 17)	26	6	
23 Oct 1989	Don't Ask Me Why (RCA CD single DACD 19)	25	6	40
29 Jan 1990	The King And Queen Of America (RCA CD single DACD 23)	29	6	
3 Apr 1990	Angel (RCA CD single DACD 21)	23	6	
25 Feb 1991	Love Is A Stranger. (RCA CD single PD 44266)—reissue—	46	3	
Nov 91	Sweet Dreams (Are Made Of This) Remix (RCA CD single PD 45032)	48	2	

The Tourists: Albums

Jun 1979	The Tourists (Logo GO 83148)	72	1	
Oct 1979	Reality Effect (Logo GO 1019)	23	16	
Oct 1980	Luminous Basement (RCA RCALP 5001)	75	1	

The Tourists: Singles

May 1979	Blind Among The Flowers (Logo GO 350)	52	5	
Jul 1979	The Loneliest Man In The World (Logo GO 360)	32	7	
Oct 1979	I Only Want To Be With You (Logo GO 370)	4	14	83
Jan 1980	So Good To Be Back Home (Logo TOUR 1)	8	9	
Sep 1980	Don't Say I Told You So (RCA TOUR 2)	40	5	

Catch: Single

Oct 1977	Borderline/Black Blood (Logo GO 103)	

Catalogue numbers and title availability are subject to change. American chart placings supplied by *Billboard* Publications.

Videos: Annie Lennox

Diva (April 1992 BMG): Why/Legend In My Living Room/Money Can't Buy It/Cold/Remember/Primitive/The Gift/Keep Young And Beautiful

Videos: Eurythmics

Sweet Dreams (1984 RCA Columbia)

Eurythmics Live (May 1988 Polygram) 90 mins

Savage (June 1988 Virgin Vision) 52 mins:Beethoven (I Love To Listen To)/I Need A Man/Brand New Day/Do You Really Want To Break Up?

We Too Are One Too (April 1990 BMG) 60 mins: We Too Are One (live)/We Too Are One (acoustic)/I Love You Like A Ball And Chain (live)/Don't Ask Me Why/How Long/You Hurt Me (And I Hate You)/(My My) Baby's Gonna Cry/We Too Are One (live)/I Need You (acoustic version)/Rudolph The Red Nosed Reindeer/The King And Queen Of America/Love Is A Stranger (live)/Sylvia (album version)/Revival/Farewell To Tarwathie/Angel/When The Day Goes Down (album version)/When The Day Goes Down (live)

Greatest Hits (April 1991 BMG): Sweet Dreams (Are Made Of This)/Love Is A Stranger/Who's That Girl?/Right By Your Side/Here Comes The Rain Again/Sexcrime (Nineteen Eighty-Four)/Julia/Would I Lie To You?/There Must Be An Angel (Playing With My Heart)/Sisters Are Doin' It For Themselves/It's Alright (Baby's Coming Back)/When Tomorrow Comes/Thorn In My Side/Miracle Of Love/Missionary Man/Beethoven (I Love To Listen To)/I Need A Man/You Have Placed A Chill In My Heart/Don't Ask Me Why/The King And Queen Of America/Angel

CHRONOLOGY

Christmas Day, 1954 Annie is born in Aberdeen
October, 1977 The Catch is formed by Annie, Dave and Peet Coombes, later to rename themselves The Tourists.
Early 1981 The Tourists split up. Dave and Annie form Eurythmics.
1981 *In The Garden* is released.
1983 *Sweet Dreams (Are Made Of This)*, the breakthrough album for Eurythmics, is released.
1983 'Who's That Girl' is released, another hit for the band.
October 1983 *Touch* album is released, consolidating popularity.
1984 The band play over 170 dates despite Annie's throat problems.
March 1984 Annie marries Krishna devotee, Radha Raman.
November, 1984 Soundtrack to *1984* is released.
February, 1985 Radha and Annie separate.
April, 1985 *Be Yourself Tonight* appears.
February, 1986 Annie duets with Chrissie Hynde at London's Royal Albert Hall.
Summer, 1986 *Revenge* is released, and Eurythmics tour for eight months.
1987 Dave is married to Siobhan Fahey of Bananarama and the band release *Savage*.
Summer, 1988 Eurythmics play at Wembley Stadium gig for ANC leader Nelson Mandela.
December, 1988 Annie's first child, Daniel, is tragically still-born.
Early 1989 Annie wins award for Best Female Singer in British pop awards.
Spring, 1989 Travels with other stars to promote Greenpeace in Russia.

September, 1989 The final Eurythmics album, *We Too Are One* is released. 65 date tour is launched to promote it.
1990 Wins British award for Best Female Singer. Annie quits pop for two years.
December 16, 1990 Annie gives birth to daughter Lola.
1991 Eurythmics' *Greatest Hits* package is released.
Early 1992 Annie launches solo career with *Diva*.
April, 1992 Annie performs at the Freddie Mercury tribute gig at Wembley.
1993 Annie is once more voted winner of Best Female Singer award at British pop ceremony. She also contributes a song to soundtrack of Coppola's *Dracula*. Second child is born—Tali.
November 1993 Dave Stewart tells British music magazine, *Vox*, that Eurythmics will never work together again. *Eurythmics Live 1983-1989* is released.

PICTURE ACKNOWLEDGMENTS

Photographs reproduced by kind permission of **London Features International**; **Pictorial Press**/Jordan,/Todd Kaplan,/Bob Leafe,/Mayer,/Terry McGough,/Brian Rasic,/Windward; **Syndicated International Network**/Peter Anderson,/David Corrio,/Peter Noble. Front cover picture: Pictorial Press

INDEX